Oliver Twist
whole heart and soul

❡

Twayne's Masterwork Studies
Robert Lecker, General Editor

Oliver Twist
whole heart and soul

¶

Richard J. Dunn

Twayne Publishers • New York
Maxwell Macmillan Canada • Toronto
Maxwell Macmillan International • New York Oxford Singapore Sydney

Twayne's Masterwork Studies No. 118

Copyright 1993 by Twayne Publishers

Twayne Publishers   Maxwell Macmillan Canada, Inc.
Macmillan Publishing Company   1200 Eglinton Avenue East
866 Third Avenue   Suite 200
New York, New York 10022   Don Mills, Ontario M3C 3N1

Macmillan Publishing Company is a part of the Maxwell Communication Group of Companies.

Library of Congress Cataloging-in-Publication Data

Dunn, Richard J., 1938–
Oliver Twist : whole heart and soul / Richard J. Dunn.
p. cm. — (Twayne's masterwork studies ; 118)
Includes bibliographical references and index.
ISBN 0-8057-9426-3 — ISBN 0-8057-8579-5 (pbk.)
1. Dickens, Charles, 1812–1870. Oliver Twist. I. Title. II. Series.
PR4567.D85   1993
823'.8—dc20   92-45051
                                                        CIP

The paper used in this publication meets the minimum requirements of American National Standard for Information Sciences—Permanence of Paper for Printed Library Materials, ANSI Z39.48-1984.

10 9 8 7 6 5 4 3 2 1 (alk. paper)

10 9 8 7 6 5 4 3 2 1 (pbk.: alk. paper)

Printed in the United States of America.

contents

illustrations

note on the references and acknowledgments

Although I identify in-text quotations from *Oliver Twist* only by chapter number, I have used and recommend the readily available Penguin edition of this and other works by Dickens. These Penguin editions provide helpful introductions and contain a number of the original illustrations. For citations from other works by Dickens, I have used these abbreviations in the text: *SB* (*Sketches by Boz*); *PP* (*Pickwick Papers*); *DC* (*David Copperfield*); *BH* (*Bleak House*); and GE (*Great Expectations*). Readers interested in the textual history of *Oliver Twist* should consult Kathleen Tillotson's introduction to the 1966 Clarendon Press edition of the novel. For consistency within the Masterwork Studies series, I have consolidated and adapted the chronologies from Bert Hornback's *Great Expectations: A Novel of Friendship* and Norman Page's *Bleak House: A Novel of Connections*.

❡

I owe much to the University of Washington students with whom I discussed *Oliver Twist* as I wrote this book: they made many helpful comments. It was in a graduate seminar during which discussion kept turning to Fagin that I realized I needed a "Fagin chapter," and some months later the analysis that constitutes Chapter 8 received a major contribution from an undergraduate, Bryan Levinson. Similarly, the germ for Chapter 9 came when I was teaching another Victorian novel: I discovered that important issues were raised when students considered various film interpretations of the work as variant readings.

At different points over the last three years I have appreciated the information only available from such colleagues as Edward

Alexander, Kathleen Blake, Joe Butwin, and Jacob Korg. As we read and reconsidered Dickens's earliest works, I have learned much about *Oliver Twist* from students Caroline Pachaud, Suzy Anger, and Shawn Soderquist. For her help with the manuscript, with clearing my calendar when necessary, and for seeing through so many projects for the past ten years, I gratefully acknowledge my assistant, Cheryl Mathiesen.

Portrait of Charles Dickens, 1839, by Daniel Maclise.

chronology: Charles Dickens's life and works

1812   Charles John Huffam Dickens born 7 February at Portsea, Hampshire, the second child and eldest son of John Dickens, a clerk in the Navy Pay Office, and his wife, Elizabeth.

1824   Family financial situation is desperate. In early February Charles begins work at Warren's Blacking Warehouse, where a Bob Fagin befriends him. John Dickens is arrested for debt and sent to the Marshalsea prison later that month. Elizabeth Dickens and the younger children move into the prison, leaving Charles in lodgings. When his father is released from prison at the end of May, Charles stops work at the warehouse and attends Wellington House Academy.

1827–1831   Dickens works as lawyer's office boy, then as a freelance shorthand reporter at Doctors' Commons.

1832   Becomes general reporter for the *True Sun*, a new evening newspaper, and a reporter for *Mirror of Parliament*, a transcript of parliamentary proceedings.

1833   In December publishes "A Dinner at Poplar Walk," the first of what in 1836 would be collected as *Sketches by Boz*.

1834   Becomes parliamentary reporter for the *Morning Chronicle*. Continues to publish sketches; uses "Boz" pseudonym for the first time.

1836	*Sketches by Boz* published. First installment of the serialized *Pickwick Papers* appears. Dickens marries Catherine Hogarth in April.
1837	First of Dickens's 10 children is born in January. In February *Oliver Twist* begins its serialization in *Bentley's Miscellany*, of which Dickens has become editor. Dickens is deeply grieved by the death of his 17-year-old sister-in-law, Mary Hogarth, in June. *Pickwick* serialization concludes in November.
1838	Serialization of *Nicholas Nickleby* begins in April. *Oliver Twist* is published in book form in November (3 vols.), but its serialization in *Bentley's Miscellany* continues until April 1839.
1839	Leaves *Bentley's Miscellany* in February. Begins work on *Barnaby Rudge*.
1840	Founds new magazine, *Master Humphrey's Clock*, wherein the serialization of *The Old Curiosity Shop* begins in April, continuing to February 1841.
1841	Serialization of *Barnaby Rudge* begins in February and continues to November. New edition of *Oliver Twist* is published with author's preface.
1842	Makes first trip to America; travel book, *American Notes*, is published in October.
1843	Serialization of *Martin Chuzzlewit* begins in January and continues to June 1844. *A Christmas Carol* is published in December.
1844	In July begins year's residency in Italy. His second Christmas book, *The Chimes*, is published in December.
1845	Begins producing and acting in amateur theatricals. *The Cricket on the Hearth*, his third Christmas book, is published in December.

1846	Edits a new newspaper, the *Daily News*, for a brief period. The travel book *Pictures from Italy* appears in May. Serialization of *Dombey and Son* begins in October. *The Battle of Life*, a fourth Christmas book, is published in December.
1848	Serialization of *Dombey and Son* concludes in April. A fifth Christmas book, *The Haunted Man*, is published in December.
1849	Serialization of *David Copperfield* begins in May.
1850	Founds and edits the weekly magazine *Household Words* (continues as editor until 1859). Cheap edition of *Oliver Twist* appears. Serialization of *David Copperfield* concludes in November.
1852	Serialization of *Bleak House* begins in March.
1853	Serialization of *Bleak House* concludes in August. Dickens gives first public reading (from *A Christmas Carol*) in December.
1854	*Hard Times* is serialized in *Household Words* from April to August.
1855	Serialization of *Little Dorrit* begins in December (concludes in June 1857).
1858	In April begins giving public readings of his work for profit. Separates from Catherine in May.
1859	Resigns as editor of *Household Words*; founds and edits a new weekly magazine, *All the Year Round*, wherein *A Tale of Two Cities* is serialized from April to November.
1860	Serialization of *Great Expectations* in *All the Year Round* begins in December (concludes in August 1861).
1864	Serialization of *Our Mutual Friend*, his last completed novel, begins in May (concludes in November 1865).
1867	Makes second trip to America for public-reading tour; publishes Charles Dickens edition of *Oliver Twist*.
1868	Adds "Sikes and Nancy" to his public readings.

1870   Serialization of *The Mystery of Edwin Drood* begins in April but is left unfinished when Dickens dies on 9 June. He is buried in Westminster Abbey on 14 June.

Literary and
Historical Context

¶

1

Dickens and Victorian England

The years of Charles Dickens's youth were expansive yet troubling ones for a nation emerging victorious from the battles of Trafalgar and Waterloo, finally ending the long Napoleonic Wars. The technologies of the industrial revolution outran social improvement, however, as England's new wealth failed to ensure a general prosperity and population growth and movement to cities produced increasingly inequitable political representation and contributed to crime and homelessness. The political economist Thomas Malthus recognized the danger signs of a population increasing much more rapidly than food supplies, and as others feared the human consequences of increasing mechanization in industry, England had new problems of crime and poverty to contend with, and in some areas these adverse conditions led to violence, with mobs destroying machines.

By the 1830s the question was not whether there would be political and social reform but just how extensive and rapid this reform would be. The landmark Parliamentary Reform Bill of 1832 produced a major redistricting of England's electorate, expanded the vote considerably, and, most importantly, set the tone for continuing attention to the problems of the nation's growth. Legislation enacted through the 1830s and 1840s concerned the poor, the constabulary, hours and terms of labor, and, most controversially, the tariffs on imported foodstuff.

These major events of the early nineteenth century had particular bearing on the life of Charles Dickens, whose largely self-
directed career parallels the collective history of an age that often
seemed to possess more good intentions and impatient energy than
certain solutions for its problems. Postreform Parliament soon
became known for its investigations, its commissions and reports,
and its readings and rereadings of proposed legislation. So too was
the early Dickens as reporter, sketcher, tale-teller, and novelist-in-
the-making, providing readers with great amounts of information.
Sketches by Boz and *The Pickwick Papers* are both filled with all
sorts of people in and around a London that teems with life. A tradition of caricature originating with William Hogarth and James
Gillray had carried forward from to George Cruikshank (who was to
illustrate *Oliver Twist*); with the popular theater, this tradition
allowed Dickens's age to hold itself up for instantaneous ridicule.

Readers of the 1830s linked Dickens's *Oliver Twist* with other
crime stories, particularly the popular fiction known as the Newgate
novel, a name derived from the eighteenth-century publication *The
Newgate Calendar; or, Malefactors' Bloody Register*. New series of
this sensational register had come out in the mid-1820s, and for
the next decade sensational stories of crime filled the press, and
hideous villains stalked the stage in Gothic plays and melodramas.
Dickens's friends William Henry Ainsworth and Edward Bulwer
(later Bulwer Lytton) were the principal Newgate novelists. It is a
small wonder, then, that in *Oliver* Dickens signals a change of
scene with tongue-in-cheek self-consciousness, claiming an obliga-
tion to alternate the tragic and comic as "in all good, murderous
melodramas" (ch. 17). In the Preface to the 1841 edition of the
novel, however, he insists that his view of the London underworld
has none of the Newgate romanticizing but comes instead from
"what I often saw and read of, in actual life around me."[1]

Just as social and political reformers attempted to establish
laws and conditions that would both respond to particular problems and serve a common good, so too did Dickens in his fiction
increasingly address the problems of crime, poverty, and sanitation.
He made the child Oliver the victim of organized charity, a harsh
master, and later of criminals. To condemn the manifest injustice
and inhumanity of his country's treatment of the innocent poor he
linked the problems of crime, hunger, and homelessness in a

crowded city with the parish workhouse and the abuse of apprentices.

For Dickens, as for many of his contemporaries distressed by present problems, the case for a better time was often the case for a past time, for the recovery of memory, imagination, and history. His favorite reading was fiction of the previous century—Henry Fielding, Tobias Smollett, and Oliver Goldsmith—authors who fostered his sharp humor and essential optimism. He also was familiar with the popular historical romances of Sir Walter Scott and the crime novels of Ainsworth and Bulwer, but unlike them Dickens celebrated childhood—recollections of a world qualitatively different from the oppressive present. Such reminiscence typically takes the form of Scrooge's first vision, the revisiting of a pleasurable earlier time, the Fezziwig Christmas party. Readers often have problems with Oliver Twist as a credible character because he is one of Dickens's celebrated children who lacks opportunity for an ideal childhood; he lives almost entirely in the present, and much of the story is about denial—first of his current identity by all who seek to use him and, second, of the past, which, in the form of an unrecognized, vengeful half-brother, threatens him for a long time.

A second important source for the Dickensian ideal is more outward than backward: a look away from the city to the country. The sites of pleasure in *Pickwick Papers* are Manor Farm and various country inns and towns, and in *Oliver Twist* the country offers its places of refuge, as is the case in so many of Dickens's works. Dickens romantically extolls nature's restorative powers, presenting an ideal of a changeless world with the timelessness of a Constable landscape or a Wordsworthian intimation of immortality.

The idealized woman is a third source and manifestation of virtue for the author and his age. Like the child, the idealized woman is indeed a problematic person because she too is abused and denied, but as image of morality and beauty, custodian of the hearth, she remains Dickens's incarnation of virtue.[2] She seems most tenable as housekeeper, as Oliver's nurse Mrs. Bedwin; she seems most untenable as unwed beauty, Rose Maylie. Although the celebration of woman was a too-prolonged and too-seldom-questioned Victorian attitude, Dickens's part in it was profoundly affected by his 17-year-old sister-in-law's death in May of 1837, while he was writing both *Pickwick* and *Oliver*.

Much, then, of what Dickens made of Victorian England in his writing was what the age itself was struggling to achieve—a sense of wholeness, an understanding of its relation to the past, and a searching for a future. How progress was to be measured, how reforms were to be continued, how people were informed and educated and entertained through the mid-nineteenth century and 34 years of Dickens's life as a writer is but part of what can be gleaned from reading his novels. The more we know of his writing, his life, and his age, the better able we are to recognize the intersections of his own interests, anxieties, and talents with those of his age, and, as we shall see, *Oliver Twist* lets us meet Dickens in the full flush of his phenomenal early success.

2

Oliver Twist's Timely Timelessness

Through his long fiction-writing career, Charles Dickens served briefly as editor of *Bentley's Miscellany* and a shorter period as editor of the *Daily News*; he founded but soon thereafter abandoned a periodical conceived as *Master Humphrey's Clock*; and he spent the final 20 years of his life as the owner and "conductor" of *Household Words*, succeeded in 1859 by *All the Year Round*. His travel books, *American Notes* and *Pictures from Italy*, as well as his collected sketches and "Uncommercial Traveller Essays" (which first appeared in *All the Year Round*), add to this body of journalistic writing, which many of today's readers too readily ignore. Through much of his journalistic writing Dickens achieved the objectives he declared in "A Preliminary Word" to *Household Words* in 1850: to "show to all, that in all familiar things, even in those which are repellent on the surface, there is Romance enough, if we find it out."[3] He repeats this commitment a few years later in his preface to *Bleak House*, commenting on his desire to dwell "upon the romantic side of familiar things."

This is no slight connection between journalist and novelist; as personal, even eccentric, as his inspiration and expression may often seem, Dickens drew constantly from what "A Preliminary Word" termed "the stirring world around us, the knowledge of many social wonders, good and evil." In doing so he is more observer than philosopher, more journalist than historian, more imaginer than explainer. All this makes the modern reader's task somewhat different from what it might be if encountering Dickens's fiction meant placing it in a history of ideas, or viewing it as historical fiction, or as accepting it as a chronicle, because Dickens shows us simultaneously his subject and his unique way of seeing it.

Certainly he passes on to us something of the spectacle he found the stirring life of his time to be, and one way we can value the permanence he gave to his vision of that life is by considering how he dealt imaginatively with some of his raw materials—the events and concerns of his day. Through its connections with public discussions of the poor law, *Oliver Twist* presents an early and impressive example of Dickens's artistic appropriation of a major current issue. We need not understand all the complexities of the poor law, for, as numerous commentators have noted, the novel does not always make clear whether it is talking about treatment of the poor before or after the poor law was passed in 1834. Even a brief glance at newspaper accounts of the debates and reactions concerning this legislation indicates the timeliness of the novel's beginning with the workhouse.

Several of the interpolated tales in early parts of *Pickwick Papers* introduced very poor people, and *Sketches by Boz* frequently featured the outcast and forlorn. When Dickens first mentioned his plan for *Oliver Twist*, he was no doubt recalling both the distress he had experienced as a child as well as the more general condition of the poor in the mid-1830s. In an autobiographical fragment composed in the 1840s and not made public before his death, Dickens told his close friend John Forster, who would be his first biographer, "But for the mercy of God, I might easily have been, for any care that was taken of me, a little robber or a little vagabond."[4] Surely, this carefully guarded attitude gave him special reason to follow discussions of the poor law and to attend especially to its provisions for children. With an advance copy of the January 1837 issue of *Bentley's Miscellany*, Dickens informed a friend that *Oliver*, which would begin the next month, was to be "my glance at the new poor Law Bill."[5]

Dickens is referring to the controversial poor-law amendment, passed finally by Parliament in 1834 and implemented in 1835. As reports of its impact and calls for its repeal appeared in newspapers and pamphlets during the following two years, debate continued over its underlying motives and immediate effects. We now can regard this legislation as the catalyst for subsequent social reform involving factory working conditions, sanitation, education, and the police force, but as the first major legislation following the 1832 Parliamentary Reform Bill, the new poor law raised much concern about public policy.

Prior to the changes in poor-law administration, the impoverished and homeless were the responsibility of local parishes and private philanthropy, and there was considerable variety of policy and practice. Some considered welfare a pernicious encouragement of idleness, an unattractive alternative to employment, and such a view characterized a distinction that would receive particular emphasis some years later in Henry Mayhew's *London Labour and the London Poor*, "a cyclopaedia of the industry, the want, and the vice of the Great Metropolis."[6] The title page for this 1861 volume pointedly separated

> THOSE THAT *WILL* WORK
> THOSE THAT *CANNOT* WORK
> THOSE THAT *WILL NOT* WORK

Mayhew's observations date primarily from the 1840s and 1850s and suggest that the earlier poor-law legislation had failed to anticipate increasing poverty. As his distinction between "deserving" and "undeserving" poor indicates, poverty continued to be considered a sin, if not a crime. We like to think we have today overcome the arbitrariness in this distinction through more careful documentation of personal need, but welfare systems constantly struggle with whether assistance to those who claim it should be immediate (and ideally temporary) or long-term, whether claimants find or exercise any right to work.

Whatever our present position, however, we can benefit from Catherine Gallagher's reminder of how persistently the Victorians divided "the working class into productive bodies out of which value is extracted and nonproductive bodies on to which it is added."[7] So viewed in the wake of Thomas Malthus's warnings about the disproportionate expansion of population and food supply, Victorian economic and political thought soon rationalized a separation of working and nonworking poor, celebrating "honest" work, or at least self-sufficiency. As Gallagher notes, Malthus's arguments placed concern for basic needs of the human body in the very center of human discourse. Just as Malthus's essay on population acknowledged what Gallagher terms "the body's power to triumph over every insolent scheme to improve, rearrange, suppress or discount it" (1987, 90), so Dickens's novel, insisting on the sturdiness of Oliver's spirit, would further make this point.

Prior to the 1834 reform, welfare in England had fallen into great disarray, and there were numerous complaints that existing systems (called "out-of-door" because they were administered from the doors of the parish rather than through a workhouse) were further discontenting and discouraging the poor. A principal objective of the poor-law amendment was to establish a "unified national system of poor relief with a strong central body administering general rules to which local bodies had to adhere."[8] The first number of *Oliver Twist* thus observes wryly, "They established the rule, that all poor people should have the alternative (for they would compel nobody, not they,) of being starved by a gradual process in the house, or by a quick one out of it" (ch. 2). The parenthetical wisecrack about compulsion reminded Dickens's first readers that the framers of the amendment saw themselves as humanitarians, political economists sharing the utilitarian principle that, left as much as possible to their own devising, a people would and could do whatever would produce "the greatest good for the greatest number."

Dickens's opposition to the new poor law was that of the humanitarian, and, as Steven Marcus has said, he "confronted injustices so directly and without equivocation, that he was able to bring before a large and extremely partisan public one of the most sensitive problems of the time, the problem of the poor."[9] Dickens's satire in the opening chapters of *Oliver* unequivocally simplified the political question of how best to legislate a poor-law reform that could be humanitarian yet discourage people from viewing welfare as the alternative to industriousness.

The status of illegitimate children proved a particularly difficult topic in the parliamentary debate. If workhouses functioned as readily available orphanages for bastards, would promiscuity be encouraged implicitly? The law placed primary responsibility on the parents of illegitimate children, but, as *Oliver Twist* shows, there often were no parents.

On the eve of the bill's final reading in the House of Lords, the bishop of Exeter proposed changes in the provisions for illegitimate children because he was concerned the new law would force the unwed mother into a workhouse, and "what was to become of her then?" He feared the workhouse would resemble "the *Inferno* of Dante, and might very properly have inscribed over it the words—'Whoever enters here leaves hope behind.'" The bishop failed to effect any change in the bill, and the *Times* looked "with heavy hearts to its future operation. The changes it will produce in what may be termed social life—for the poor surely are a part of society—are of the most fearful and ominous kind. The poor, whether infirm or in need of employment, are to be fed, clothed, and housed, by strangers . . . [and] the connexion between the poor and their neighbors is broken."[10] This perfectly predicts the fate of Oliver's mother, who, when found lying in the street, is brought "by the overseer's order" to the workhouse, where she dies soon after giving birth to her son. Echoing his contemporaries' concerns about the fate of bastard children and the absence of neighborly aid, Dickens describes the death of Oliver's mother as strangers "chafed her breast, hands, and temples" and "talked of hope and comfort. They had been strangers too long" (ch. 1). Introduced without family, Oliver falls "into his place at once—a parish child—the orphan of a workhouse—the humble half-starved drudge, to be cuffed and buffeted through the world—despised by all, and pitied by none" (ch. 1).

Dickens's criticisms of the workhouses are mainly of the insufficiency of care, lack of adequate food, and absence of compassion, and his accounts certainly do not exaggerate frequent newspaper reports about workhouse conditions. These include instances of corruption, mismanagement, and brutality by authorities and contracted providers. Oliver, hungry and abused, would have been a familiar figure to Dickens's audience.

From the parliamentary debates in 1834 through the weeks preceding the serialization of *Oliver Twist* in February 1837, reports in the London *Times* anticipate many of Dickens's concerns about the treatment of the poor. Dickens had just begun writing sketches in his spare time and had already been a parliamentary reporter on the staff of the *Morning Chronicle* while the poor-law amendment was being considered in 1834. If he wrote for newspapers about the poor law, none of this work has been identified; in the pages of the *Times*, however, we find a rich contemporary context for *Oliver's* attention to this issue.

When the poor-law amendment was passed by the House of Commons the *Times* remarked that already more than 100 petitions had been made against it, and the paper commented that never had there been penned "a more dangerous, a more mischievous, or a more unconstitutional measure." The same editorial suggested the reintroduction of Jonathan Swift's *Modest Proposal* as an alternative, for it might be more humane to resort to cannibalism than to legislate slow starvation (*Times*, 7/1/1834). This Swiftian note sounds more extensively through the opening chapters of Dickens's novel as he satirizes the "logic" of keeping paupers on minimal rations.

When the proposed amendment went to the House of Lords, the lord chancellor, Henry Brougham, praised it as the means of combating "all the evils . . . of pampered idleness," and he hailed it as model legislation by "theorists and visionaries, and . . . political economists," citing in particular its consistency with the social theories of Thomas Malthus (*Times*, 7/22/1834). The utilitarian principles of Malthus and Jeremy Bentham were frequent targets for Dickens, most prominently in *Hard Times*, his 1850s attack on self-serving economic and educational practices and theories. In *Oliver Twist* he effectively satirizes Brougham's assumptions: "Although Oliver had been brought up by philosophers he was not theoretically acquainted with the beautiful axiom that self-preservation is the first law of nature" (ch. 10)—and often scorns "philosophers," having little use for theory inconsistent with practice (mere rhetoric and display), all of which is the essence of "Bumbledom." Bumble, the workhouse beadle, is thus an example of vanity and selfishness, gluttony and greed, but he also is the functionary of the institution, the proof that self-interest is not only tolerated but promoted by the authorities. Here Dickens's satire gets to the central problem presented by the utilitarian idealists. Emerging from Enlightenment expectations that self and social love could be the same, that self-regulation made sense in the long run, "self-preservation" seemed less problematic to the political economists than it was to Dickens, whose Oliver Twist makes a clear case that officialdom cannot have its cake and share it too.

This is the point that most directly links Dickens's attention to the poor law and to the criminal world. Just as Bumble regales himself and ostentatiously flaunts all the signs of his beadledom, and just as he takes careful stock of Mrs. Corney's possessions before proposing, so too does Fagin hoard his booty. His instruction to a new member of his gang becomes the novel's most ironic "philosophic" statement about self-interest:

> To keep my little business all snug, I depend upon you. The first is your number one, the second my number one. The more you value your number one, the more careful you must be of mine; so we come at last to what I told you at first—that a regard for number one holds us all together, and must do so, unless we would all go to pieces in company. (ch. 43)

Fagin's "little business" is at this point fast going to pieces, for the gallows he approaches stands as a mute reminder of the terror of the single digit, in Fagin's words, "an ugly finger-post, which points out a very short and sharp turning that has stopped many a bold fellow's career" (ch. 43).

For Dickens the ideal is community, not self-sustenance, and just as Daniel O'Connell objected in the House of Commons to the poor law's doing "away with personal feelings and connexions" (*Times*, 7/1/1834), so in his novel would Dickens lambaste

> the little code of laws which certain profound and sound-urging philosophers have laid down as the mainsprings of all Nature's deeds and actions: the said philosophers very wisely reducing the good lady's proceedings to matters of maxim and theory: and, by a very neat and pretty compliment to her exalted wisdom and understanding, putting entirely out of sight any considerations of heart, or generous impulse and feeling. (ch. 12)

The newspaper's notice of abuses well prepared Dickens's readers for the conditions he would attribute to his fictional workhouse. There were cases of collusion between parochial surgeons and overseers, instances of virtual imprisonment prohibiting paupers from attending their chosen places of worship. An article appearing in January 1837 points to a prototypic Mrs. Mann, a Kentish schoolmistress administering "to the child what would be too nauseating to describe or even to mention," and notes also that a baker for the Grantham workhouse had put soap into bread he supplied for paupers (*Times*, 1/21/1837).

Coincident with the appearance of *Oliver Twist* in February 1837, the *Times* reprinted the Bradford *Observer* account of an impassioned protest against the poor law by the Reverend G. S. Bull. Bull's remarks remarkably parallel the view Dickens was taking of workhouse management and conditions. Like Dickens, Bull resented the absolute power of absent commissioners, under whom guardians "dare not give one spoonful of porridge more to the inmates of a workhouse than their three great masters choose to order." Bull itemized the weekly rations sanctioned for the workhouse and "produced great sensation" by exhibiting to his audience the daily ration, *one-seventh* of the weekly allotment of

42 oz. bread	24 oz. potatoes
15 ditto of beef	$4 1/2$ pints of Soup
8 ditto of cheese	$19 1/2$ of Gruel

A few weeks before the *Times* published this information, Dickens told his publisher that he had "hit upon a capital notion for myself, and one which will bring Cruikshank [his illustrator] out" (*Letters*, 1: 224). His notion was the germ of the famous illustration of Oliver asking for more gruel, and it struck the keynote not simply of his satire against the poor law but also of his continuing concern for its victims:

> "Please, sir, I want some more."
> The master was a fat, healthy man; but he turned very pale. He gazed in stupefied astonishment on the small rebel for some seconds; and then clung for support to the copper. The assistants were paralyzed with wonder; the boys with fear.
> "What!" said the master at length, in a faint voice.
> "Please, sir," replied Oliver, "I want some more."
> The master aimed a blow at Oliver's head with the ladle; pinioned him in his arms; and shrieked aloud for the beadle. (ch. 2)

Convinced that this rebellious act augers Oliver's destiny to be hanged, the parish board orders "instant confinement; and a bill was next morning pasted on the outside of the gate, offering a reward of five pounds to anybody who would take Oliver Twist off the hands of the parish" (ch. 2). Here, too, is a detail Dickens and Rev. Bull both target, for in the same speech mentioning the rationed gruel, Bull spoke also against the "slave-trade" of sending out paupers as apprentices.

As do Bull's, other protests of the poor law resound with Dickensian extremes of indignation and of sympathy for paupers. Under the heading "The Horrible Working of the Poor Law Amendment Act" the *Times* tells of a 14-year-old girl given asylum "by a very benevolent" lady, but the girl had suffered too long and died of starvation. Such contemporary reports carry the sting of the novel's satirical account of the philosopher eager to prove his theory about horses living without eating had his own horse not died unexpectedly when the ration was "down to a straw a day" (ch. 2). In the same vein, the reporter noted that the girl's death had proved the "well-known fact, that long-protracted hunger will so far destroy the natural functions of the stomach, that in some instances no care or attention can possibly restore its healthy or natural tone" (*Times*, 2/8/1837).

On 15 February 1837 four-and-a-half columns of the *Times* featured excerpts from an 1834 pamphlet, "The Cause of the Poor Defended against the Poor Law Commission." Reappearing at the time Dickens's novel was beginning its serialization, the commentary could well be describing Dickens's hero:

> Alas! if it could be seen how, step by step, goaded by the shafts of necessity, many a bright soul has become dim, and many a virtuous disposition depraved, which happier circumstances would have carried on in a course of benevolence and honour—how would the consideration lead us to thank God that we have not been exposed to the same rough tide of circumstance—how would it disease us to look with an eye of sorrow rather than of anger on our unhappy brethren, and instead of venting against them the curses of men, to shed over them the tears of angels! (*Times*, 2/15/1837)

Often it seems that, for Dickens, angel tears, taking the form of such sympathies as Rose Maylie's for the doomed Nancy in *Oliver Twist*, are the only conceivable responses to a cursed human condition. Such emotional moments may express necessary feelings but seldom can carry on practically "in a course of benevolence and honour," and the pamphleteer continues, sensitive to the sort of criticism Dickens would receive from those who find him too sentimental and idealistic:

> Perhaps I may be deemed romantic for the feelings which my conscience compels me to express on this important subject; but let him that so judges consider how far all the piety, virtue, and humanity, are regarded as romantic in this wicked world; and how far any thing is looked upon as rational to its inhabitants, but what is available to the purposes of pride, vanity, and ambition. (*Times*, 2/15/1837)

Sharing Dickens's faith in "the principle of Good surviving through every adverse circumstance, and triumphing at last" (1841 Preface), the writer argues that although "human nature must be acknowledged to be depraved, it still possesses sufficient integrity and intelligence, and enough of the principle of self-preservation, to pursue in general the safe, reputable, and advantageous course of innocence, virtue, and industry" (*Times*, 2/15/1837). As we have seen, Dickens has some doubts about self-preservation as a motive, and his adherence to the idea of a persevering goodness is more collective than individual, or at least more innate than willed.

In addition to the poor law, *Oliver Twist* refers to a number of other topical matters, especially crime and law enforcement, and in at least one instance Dickens sought out a particular prototype. To describe accurately the fictional magistrate Fang, Dickens asked a friend to smuggle him into the Hatton Garden office of a magistrate named Mr. Laing (*Letters*, 1: 267). And for a more kindly case study, he simply appropriated the name of Oliver's principal benefactor from John Brownlow, a friend who worked at a nearby foundling hospital and who himself happened to have written a novel about a fortunate foundling.[11]

For Fagin and his gang, Dickens drew on many possible sources—direct observations and written accounts of London's criminal gangs; previous fiction such as Henry Fielding's *Life of Jonathan Wild* and possibly Daniel Defoe's *Moll Flanders*; and boyhood experience that subjectively fused senses of guilt, poverty, and criminal desire, if not criminal conduct. Gangs and police efforts against them were matters of frequent concern during the 1830s. After the establishment of London's Metropolitan Police force in the early 1830s, a constabulary commission was directed to determine how best to establish a similar force in the countryside. Its survey of the "state of crime and the means available for its prevention or repression,"[12] published in 1839, retrospectively substantiates many of the criminal activities in Dickens's novel. The report describes the training of young thieves, boys beginning criminal life at the age of seven or eight, instructed through games with "one or two pals or confederates." The report even suggests that these pals may be such free spirits as Dickens's Artful Dodger, for it mentions that, when faced with transportation as punishment, the child convict is "soon rallied by his more jocular and less thinking companions."

The report claims that the pickpockets' fences "for the most part, are Jews," and "now and then, when an old thief is present where young ones are, these practise their art upon one another." The report's concern about London criminals moving through the less well policed countryside, breaking into houses, includes a detailed description of such. As does Sikes in the novel, the real-life housebreakers would make use of a boy, putting him in a window, where if caught he might begin to cry, because "tears have a mighty effect, thieves say, on honest people; some good-natured dame in the family pities the boy, attributes all the blame to some unknown naughty bad man." Although wounded and unconscious, Oliver evokes just this response when he has been abandoned by Sikes after the aborted effort to rob a country house.

Another parallel between novel and commission report concerns women in the criminal world. The report confirms Sikes's premise that they cannot be trusted, especially if they drink, because then they begin to boast of their men's feats and "the conversation is overheard, and the necessary information is given to cause the apprehension of the offenders."

The report amply authenticates *Oliver Twist*'s underworld, and some of its observations alert us to the similar attitudes authorities were taking to poverty and crime. The commission insisted that the motive for crime was less often "the pressure of unavoidable want or destitution" than the "temptation of obtaining property with a less degree of labour than by regular industry," an explanation resembling those which saw poverty as the consequence of laziness. Furthermore, the commissioners regarded the criminal as irredeemable: "It is an aphorism currently received amongst many of the officers engaged in the administration of the law, 'once a thief, always a thief.'" Noting the pride of the expert thief, his goal to reach "the top of the tree in the profession," the report, like the novel, presents the criminal as the dauntless entrepreneur, whose principal concern is number one.

Reading *Oliver Twist* with some awareness of its original public's interest in and awareness of the conditions of the poor and the criminal allows us to glimpse the passing life to which Dickens gave lasting attention. He did not simply use a hot topic to promote sales, to make the fiction seem truthful, to provide posterity with yet more information about an age always eager to document itself. Rather, with the materials we have noted, he constructed a telling satire of the most vulnerable aspects of the new poor law, a fascinating presentation of desperate lives, at his best showing how his people see one another and their predicaments or at least how, by hook or by crook, they cope. A careful reading of this novel and other Dickens works lets us share both his ways of seeing and those of his characters, and it is his characters' "reading" of one another and their world that enlivens his fiction and makes us look again at what we might have ignored or only taken for granted as familiar things.

3

The Importance of Oliver Twist

Oliver Twist persists as one of those classic stories with appeal for young and old, for readers simply enjoying the story and students considering its importance as a novel addressing major concerns of the Victorians, for those interested in the impetus it gave to the start of Dickens's phenomenal career. For some readers, it may be the book's more sensational elements that seem most important—the melodramatic overstatements of sentimentality or terror—or perhaps the fairy-tale quality of its plot line, punctuated with nightmarish encounters. Others may insist, as did Dickens in the preface to the novel's 1841 edition, that the book is important because it presents such a realistic, uncompromising account of early Victorian England. Certainly many of the social problems of that time remain so, with little real change, in our time. Many may simply remember the novel's most remarkable characters—Bumble the beadle, the Artful Dodger, or Fagin—or recall its most memorable scenes—Oliver asking for "more," his meeting with the Dodger, the intrusion of Fagin and Sikes into his new life.

What is important about this novel endures for any reader through generations of readings. *Oliver Twist* well represents what is of continuing importance about Dickens's art. The ingenuity and the energy of his imagination carries forward directly in his narration and characterization. Always with us is the storyteller's imagination, capable of depicting for us the most extraordinary aspects of ordinary experience. For example, the narrator lets us see just how cruelly distorted the workhouse board's view is when he remarks that they thought paupers found the workhouse "a brick and mortar elysium" (ch. 2). Bumble, articulating self-delusions in virtually every word, is funny and very imaginative, as is Fagin in the games by which he both entertains and instructs his boys. Equally imaginative, but always more sinister, the murderer Bill Sikes personifies the novel's darkest fears. Here, then, in the imaginings of characters and the verbal dynamics of the narrator, Dickens has, as he realized, poured "whole heart and soul" into *Oliver Twist*. It is no wonder the novel has such intensities and anxieties, such abundance of good humor and hopefulness.

It is important that we understand just why all this happened, just what about the novel stimulated it, because the novel's importance is such a continuing story. Dickens is a most dramatic novelist, unsurprising because of his life-long love of theater, his activity in amateur theatricals, and his public readings. The dramatic elements of his writing are its visual and vocal sharpness. Readers "see" as they "hear" Dickens. The visual was reinforced by the illustrations that accompanied each monthly number (and that gave the cues for casting and set design for so many stage and screen versions of Dickens's novels). The vocal element was perhaps more emphatic for Victorian readers, who frequently read novels aloud, than to more recent readers, but the self-dramatizing speech of a Bumble or a Fagin becomes all the more prominent on the stage or screen.

Through popular adaptations *Oliver Twist* has reached many people who have never read the novel, and a number of people may have read the novel because they have seen one of its adaptations. However one comes to *Oliver Twist*, it remains a work that stimulates the imagination as it makes its case for the title character. Like those with whom Oliver struggled, readers need to see him, as Dickens saw him, as an innocent whose face reflects the goodness among us and whose experience represents the precariousness of this goodness. Wholeheartedly incorporating so much of Dickens's imaginative energy, *Oliver Twist* remains a powerful argument for wholeness of heart and soul in our world.

4

How the Novel Was Received

It is not uncommon to find greatly popular works of nineteenth-century fiction receiving serious critical attention and also attaining almost instant status as "classics." With Dickens's novels this is certainly true, but to understand the enduring popularity and continuing critical acclaim, we must realize that Dickens's novels—through the months of serial publication, years of reprintings and collected editions; through piracies and adaptations and the versions Dickens himself read publicly—came repeatedly before audiences, even during his lifetime. Following a work's serial publication (all his books first appeared in parts published before he had finished writing the entire novel), Dickens's subsequent prefaces, revisions, and responses to unauthorized theatrical adaptation become part of the story of *Oliver Twist*'s reception.

Commenting on Dickens's first four books—*Sketches by Boz, Pickwick Papers, Oliver Twist, Nicholas Nickleby*—the *Edinburgh Review* in October 1838 proclaimed him the most popular writer of his day, acknowledging not only the impressive sales figures but also the dramatic adaptations, translations, and parodies of his fiction. Dickens's success for this reviewer rested on his originality, remarkable powers of observation, "comprehensive spirit of humanity," and great skill in communicating, whether he is writing with exuberant humor or pathos.[13] This early reviewer expresses the prevailing grounds for Dickens's instant and continuing reputation, and some of his observations apply to popular fiction more generally. The remarkable success of Dickens in many ways resembles that of some of the most popular authors of our time. Readers found in his early work the ingredients that he would mix in varied recipes for nearly 35 years, during which there was rarely a time when a new or a reissued Dickens story was not before the public. Like most of Dickens's fiction, *Oliver Twist* was adapted for the stage even before its serial run ended, and without Dickens's permission or consultation. There was an unauthorized American edition, and by 1845 the novel had been translated into German, Italian, Dutch, French, Hungarian, Swedish, and Polish, and Dickens received no royalties for any foreign editions.

Oliver ran serially in *Bentley's Miscellany*, from February 1837 through April 1839 (no installment of the novel appeared in the June 1837, October 1837, or September 1838 numbers, however). This was an incredibly busy and productive time for Dickens: through November 1837 he was finishing *Pickwick* and in April 1838 began publishing *Nicholas Nickleby*; for the next year both it and *Oliver* were appearing. Also during this period a new publisher, Chapman and Hall, was reissuing in monthly parts (November 1837 to June 1839) Dickens's first published writings, *Sketches by Boz*, which had been collected in book form in 1836. With overlap and reissue the publication history of Dickens's early writing can be confusing, but the public found his work constantly before them, and by the time *Oliver*'s serial parts were first combined in book form, the title page dropped the "Boz" pseudonym in favor of "By Charles Dickens. Author of *The Pickwick Papers*."

During its 24 months of serialization, *Oliver* attracted frequent and repeated attention by reviewers, and in her listing of early reviews, Kathleen Tillotson finds that it averaged five reviews a month.[14] Nineteenth-century reviewers often said little but included long passages they thought representative of their readings. Few speculated on the serial's direction, even though they often remarked on the particular demands of this relatively new form of publication. In retrospect we realize that Dickens could benefit from the frequency and number of reviews accompanying his serials, for it was possible for him to adjust the course and tone of his work as he received reactions to it.

A few of the reviews of *Oliver Twist* are reprinted in Philip Collins's *Dickens: The Critical Heritage*, and many more are listed and annotated in David Paroissien's *Oliver Twist: An Annotated Bib-liography*. The reviews were largely favorable, recognizing the descriptive powers Dickens had already well displayed in *Sketches*, the eye for the ludicrous that had distinguished *Pickwick Papers*, and his role "as a moralist and reformer of cruel abuses" (Collins, 73).

From the first, commentators on *Oliver* identified features that have interested later generations of readers. They found in it "sympathy with all things good and beautiful in human nature, the perception of character, the pathos, and accuracy of description."[15] Like so much of Dickens's writing, the novel seems original despite some superficial resemblance to previous or contemporary treatments of similar subjects; thus the November 1837 *Atlas* reviewer finds more power in the novel's terror that "in the whole range of English fiction."[16] In the June 1839 *Quarterly* conservative reviewer Richard Ford acknowledges Dickens's popularity but clearly states major objections to the novel. He grants that Dickens seems "born with an organic bump for distinct observation of men and things" but "fails whenever he attempts to write for effect" and "vulgar when treating on subjects which are avowedly vulgar." Ford's strongest objection is to Dickens's focus on "the outcasts of humanity, who do their dirty work in work, pot, and watch houses, to finish on the Newgate drop." Politically he resents Dickens's treatment of the poor-law and workhouse system: "The abuses he ridicules are not only exaggerated, but in nineteen cases out of twenty do not at all exist. Boz so rarely mixes up politics, or panders to vulgar prejudices about serious things, that we regret to see him joining an outcry which is partly factious, partly sentimental, partly interested."[17]

The political bias of this viewpoint is evident when we contrast it with an opinion more acceptable to Dickens, that of the radical politician Sir Francis Burdett, who in 1838 had told his daughter that he had found Dickens's novel "very interesting, very painful, very disgusting, & as the Old Woman at Edinburgh, on hearing a preacher on the sufferings of Jesus Christ, said Oh dear I hope it isn't true. Whether anything like it exists or no I mean to make inquiry for it is quite dreadful, and to Society in this country, most disgraceful" (*Letters*, 1: 472n).

Dickens's characters attracted much immediate interest, and like generations of later readers the earlier reviewers found his rogues and villains more credible than his good people. Responding positively to the power with which Dickens portrayed Nancy, Sikes, and Fagin, the *Quarterly* regarded Oliver as an improbable character, "represented to be a pattern of modern excellence, guileless himself, and measuring others by his own innocence."

Only a few of the earlier reviewers could find much that was imagining or imaginative about Oliver himself, but after meeting a number of the more interesting children from Dickens's subsequent novels, readers might well have remembered Oliver's as a familiar situation for Dickens's fictional children—innocents beset by all sorts of uncertainties, young people who, like Dickens himself, felt deeply and had often to make their ways determinedly through difficulty.

Dickens's interest in the child, like his more specific attention to poverty, crime, and sanitation, is a major factor in his continuing popularity, because it was his particular genius to be at once topical and universal. By satirizing the real-life magistrate Mr. Laing in *Oliver*'s Mr. Fang, and by speaking of the workhouse, the pauper's hovel, or the thieves' den in terms as explicit as any journalistic report, he was speaking to contemporaries about his own world. His way of speaking, his penchant for the "telling" detail, the primary attitude or feeling, the sense of atmosphere—all this captured pain or joy, the hope or hopelessness of human life under duress or in moments of release. This imaginative power Dickens shares with Shakespeare, for both particularize and immortalize through the language of their many memorable characters—imagined beings who, like Bumble or Falstaff, Fagin or Shylock, Nancy or Ophelia, express themselves most imaginatively. As surely as we sense much of Dickens's imagination in many of his characters so too do we find his imagined beings so credible that we have come to describe real people resembling them as somehow "out of Dickens."

Often Dickens is described in seemingly oxymoronic terms as a "popular classic." This phrase can be troublesome if we are too bothered by Dickens's unevennesses, especially by writing that often was necessarily hasty, even improvised, and in early works sometimes clumsily handled. It can be troublesome, too, if we take the high culture position that anything popular cannot have much esthetic value, or if, on the other hand, we define "popular" by the lowest criteria of Dickens's or our own time. Just as we have a broad range of "popular" fiction today, some of it most unimaginative and formulaic, so in Dickens's day were there standard novels of low life and crime, and especially of religious and moral instruction. The Dickens who stands out, then and now, is a writer who animates and enlivens, gives unique expression to what in other hands would remain dull and ordinary.

After its serial run, *Oliver Twist* underwent more than usual revision and republication. Five substantive editions produced five further stages of revision. After the monthly numbers came the first collected edition, another monthly-part publication (this time in 10 parts), a single-volume edition of 1846 (for which there were many textual revisions), the Cheap edition of 1850, and the Charles Dickens edition of 1867. Relatively few changes were made for this last edition during Dickens's lifetime, but in response to the complaint of a Jewish friend, Dickens did delete or alter many of the references to Fagin as "the Jew." Granted, many of these revisions are important only to those interested in the process of Dickens's composing and publishing, but as each edition came forward, Dickens continued to treat *Oliver* as a work-in-progress.

Beginning in the early 1850s Dickens adapted parts of his novels for public readings. He had once considered becoming a professional actor, directed and played in amateur theatricals for most of his life, and thus the term *readings* hardly describes the one-man show he produced as he performed the roles of multiple characters as well as narrator. At first he gave readings for charity, but he soon realized their personal profitability and occasion for furthering the close relationship he felt with his readers. As he recalled, he had begun the readings "sustained by the hope that I could drop into some hearts, some new expression of the meaning of my books, that would touch them in a new way."[18] He also found himself particularly touched by this experience, for it intensified his authorial presence: "so real are my fictions to myself, that after these hundreds of nights, I come with a feeling of perfect freshness . . . and laugh and cry with my hearers, as if I had never stood there before" (Kaplan, 507). Here Dickens not only speaks to the emotional satisfaction he took in his performances, the life-sustaining Scheherazade on stage, but he also acknowledges that, having attracted a public through long-running serials and through the publication of story after story, he could extend this relationship through public performance. Often when he wrote, as his family observed, he would be in dialogue with his characters, smiling, gesturing, muttering to them. With the readings, this performance turned outward, and by all reports of its vitality seems indisputable proof that the fiction was Dickens himself.

Dickens's most impassioned public reading was adapted from *Oliver Twist.* The "Sikes and Nancy" reading of his farewell series beginning in 1868 became his most frequent and strenuous performance. Although he wanted "something very passionate and dramatic," he was uncertain about its effects, and could not have been surprised when a friend warned, "You may rely upon it that if one woman cries out when you murder the girl, there will be a contagion of hysteria all over the place."[19] "Sikes and Nancy" certainly had the passionate effect Dickens intended, exciting and exhausting him in the process.

Victorians loved extremes, as a glance at popular theater, sensational fiction, and the daily press reminds us. Dickens's works, most particularly those of the late 1850s and 1860s, often capitalized on the violent and terrible. Readers of *A Tale of Two Cities, Great Expectations,* and *Our Mutual Friend* would not find the "Sikes and Nancy" reading, intense as it was, radically different from these "darker" novels, and the focus on crime and guilt would be primary in *The Mystery of Edwin Drood,* left unfinished at Dickens's death in 1870.

The reception, then, of *Oliver Twist* during Dickens's lifetime was affected by his reissue of the work, his comments about it, and his adaptation of it for the public reading. Much of the novel's popularity has continued since Dickens's death, with further stage versions and many film and television adaptations. As with many Dickens characters and phrases, incidents such as Oliver's asking for "more" and pronouncements by Bumble, the Artful Dodger, and Fagin seem to have found life apart from the pages of the novel. And, like most Dickens's novels, *Oliver Twist* continues to appeal to different readers at different times of their lives. He is a writer for adults as well as children; he is a writer of his times but also for his times; he is a writer who both reveals and conceals the complexities of his mind and heart; and he is a writer who can both distress and delight readers with stories that succeed despite loose ends, excesses, and improbabilities.

Dickens studies in the latter half of the twentieth century have tended to concentrate on the later Dickens, the more mature writer often associated with Kafka and Dostoyevski than with Dickens's contemporary English novelists or his favorite eighteenth-century writers, Fielding and Smollett. Several important modern studies have nonetheless found much in this novel to interest readers of Dickens's later works. J. Hillis Miller in *Charles Dickens: The World of His Novels* (1958) challenges the assumptions of many readers about the title character's lack of self-awareness and argues that he comes to a spontaneous and simple "all-embracing . . . conscious-ness of his total solitude."[20] Much of my own view—that Oliver's security comes from an indefinite past that nonetheless becomes more accessible in the course of his life—grows from Miller's dis-cussion of the novel's claustrophobic present time. Unlike Miller, however, I believe that it is others' views of Oliver, rather than his sense of himself, that Dickens stresses, because the focus remains on him as a representative child—more on what the world makes of Oliver than on what he makes of it.

In his influential *Dickens: From Pickwick to Dombey* (1965), Steven Marcus well describes the ways in which *Oliver Twist* becomes a major text in the literature of social injustice. Marcus is especially helpful in identifying the novel's most intense energies as those "in which the documentary impulse becomes an imaginative power" (1965, 77). Marcus writes with particular interest about the characterization of Fagin—a fascination I share.

By far the most comprehensive and challenging reading of *Oliver Twist* is Robert Tracy's "'The Old Story' and Inside Stories: Modish Fiction and Fictional Modes in Oliver Twist" (1988). More than most commentators, Tracy considers the important role of George Cruikshank, Dickens's famous illustrator, and he notes many parallels between this and other novels of the day—parallels further described in Kathryn Chittick's more recent study, *Dickens and the 1830s* (1990).

These and other modern critics have had few divisions of opinion about the novel's importance to Dickens's prospering ca-reer, to the development of socially conscious fiction, or to the enduring popular fascination with crime and punishment. What argument there has been has involved the credibility of the novel's insistence on the triumph of Oliver's innocence. Certainly many of the novel's presentations of goodness—be it Oliver's, that of many of the women characters, or that of the patriarchal benefactor Brownlow—are unconvincing when compared with the imaginative energies projected from the novel's underworld. Here there is ground to agree with Graham Greene's sense of the novel's divided worlds.[21]

The measure of the success of *Oliver Twist* is to be taken in the terms by which Dickens infused his own wholeheartedness into the imaginative life of his characters and into his highly visual portrayal of early Victorian England. Once wholly engaged, such imaginative existence becomes protean within the covers of Dickens's work and beyond his and others' adaptations of the novel.

A Reading

¶

5

Wholeheartedness and Wholeness

At work in late January 1837 on the second monthly installment of his new novel, Dickens enthusiastically informed Richard Bentley, his publisher, "I have thrown my whole heart and soul into Oliver Twist, and most confidently believe he will make a feature in the work, and be very popular" (*Letters*, 1: 227). As editor of *Bentley's Miscellany* he wanted to assure Bentley that the magazine was off to a good start and would benefit from featuring *Oliver Twist*. Dickens's letters through the two years when he was writing the novel seldom distinguish between the work as a whole and the title character, and similarly he spoke of later works as "Dombey," or "Copperfield," or "Little Dorrit." We therefore should take him primarily to mean that he finds himself caught up heart and soul in his new novel, that the writing is going well, and that he is very confident of pleasing his readers.

Because this novel has many parallels with important parts of Dickens's earlier life, recollecting especially his work in the blacking warehouse, he literally was possessed, whole heart and soul, with it well before the writing began. By the time he started *Oliver* Dickens had won great popularity with *Pickwick Papers* and had every reason for confidence as he pushed forward with new work that took him in two important new directions—a child hero and a controversial contemporary subject. A few days after declaring his excitement to Bentley, he sent another correspondent an advance copy of "the forthcoming Miscellany [*sic*], with my glance at the new poor Law

31

Bill" (*Letters*, 1: 231). The "heart and soul" of Dickens's work as writer, in his fiction and journalism, and of many of his avocations as well, is his passionate humanitarianism. It takes many forms, but it focuses repeatedly on the suffering of women and children and such deserving but downtrodden characters as the *Christmas Carol*'s Bob Cratchitt. In expressing and calling for sympathy for such people, Dickens ranges from sentimental effusions over their inherent worth to satirical attacks on their persecutors, be they individuals or institutions.

Especially in such later books as *Bleak House* he rages more prophetically, to warn that the London slum "Tom-all-Alone's" has its revenge by propagating infection and contagion:

> There is not an atom of Tom's slime, not a cubic inch of any pestilential gas in which he lives, not one obscenity or degrada-tion about him, not an ignorance, not a wickedness, not a brutal-ity of his committing, but shall work its retribution, through every order of society, up to the proudest of the proud, and to the high-est of the high. Verily, what with tainting, plundering, and spoiling, Tom has his revenge. (*BH*, ch. 46)

Few of Dickens's descriptions of slums in *Oliver Twist* so vividly express the passion of his social commentary. This *Bleak House* passage reminds us that Dickens's much earlier commitment of his whole heart and soul to his writing was not the mere headiness of the young writer who had found sudden fame with his first book but rather a more enduring emotional involvement with his fictional world. On visiting the Dickens house one evening when Dickens was writing *Oliver Twist* in a corner of the drawing room, the fiancé of Dickens's sister noted, "It was interesting to watch, upon the sly, the mind and the muscles working (or, if you please, *playing*) in company, as new thoughts were being dropped upon the paper. And to note the working brow, the set of mouth, with the tongue tightly pressed against the closed lips, as was his habit."[23]

Dickens seldom wrote in the company of others, but here we gain a rare glimpse of his powers of concentration. So engaged, it is no wonder that Dickens would find himself as much subject to as inventor of the evolving story, for as he later told a curious reviewer, he, "like most authors," could take pleasure in what he had written, finding a particular "passage a good one *when* I wrote it, certainly, and I felt it strongly (as I do almost every word I put on paper) *while* I wrote it, but how it came I can't tell. It came like all my other ideas, such as they are, ready made to the point of the pen—and down it went" (*Letters*, 1: 403).

Both these accounts suggest that writing came easily to Dickens, that it was a sort of play that he delighted in, yet a strong, even desperate, work ethic emerges when in later years Dickens tried to account for his success. His one novelist-hero, David Copperfield, takes pride in perseverance, patience, and continuous energy, which he found to be strong parts of his character:

> I never could have done what I have done, without the habits of punctuality, order, and diligence, without the determination to concentrate myself on one object at a time, no matter how quickly its successor should come upon its heels. . . . Whatever I have tried to do in life, I have tried with all my heart to do well; that whatever I have devoted myself to, I have devoted myself to completely; that in great aims and in small I have always been thoroughly in earnest. (*DC*, ch. 42)

This so essentially Victorian credo may seem to contradict Dickens's more private declaration of the writer being subject to the dictates of imagination as well his friend's account of his "playing" as he wrote. How, we may well wonder, can the writer both be so earnest in his social criticism, so affected by his sense of childhood shame, and yet so freely fanciful? The question is as important to our understanding of what Dickens produced as to our sense of how he worked, because over the long course of any single novel, as well as of his long career, Dickens sustained yet varied his imaginative intensity as he mixed the humorous and serious. He could never have succeeded as a serial writer without a strong work ethic, but a work ethic alone might have resulted in more repetitive, pedestrian writing. As David Copperfield's self-revelation indicates, it was not just sustained hard work but the capacity to focus intently as he moved from one fictional objective to another that distinguished his work.

Too often we associate Victorian earnestness merely with a repressive and unimaginative morality, but in Dickens's case earnestness characteristically manifested itself as total involvement in the life of his fiction. When we find Dickens simply "too much," hyper in his presence as narrator, unrestrained in his laughter or tears, exhausting in his excitements, we understand the risk of this manner of writing. So much wholeheartedness may seem esthetically unwholesome because it celebrates life, especially the imaginative life of the novelist, more than art, from which we rightly or wrongly demand coherence or "objectivity." Thus a principal risk in Dickens is that of self-centeredness and self-indulgence. In the course of his early successes he privately referred to himself as the "Inimitable Boz," and the true force of his power projects both to his most memorable characters and to his most appreciative readers. For just as a Fagin or an Artful Dodger becomes an incarnation of the author's distinctive imagination, so too may readers begin to see some of their world as yet another Dickens novel. The wholehearted intensity of Dickens's imagination is more communal than solipsistic, more socializing than self-indulgent. In introducing his new weekly periodical, *Household Words*, in 1850, Dickens best expressed his objective of cherishing "that light of Fancy which is inherent in the human breast" so that even the world's "hardest workers" will find "that their lot is not necessarily a moody, brutal fact, excluded from the sympathies and graces of imagination."

For Dickens "wholeheartedness" certainly involved far more than the passion he gave to writing the early parts of *Oliver Twist*; it is a principle he followed throughout his career. Most particularly for *Oliver*, Dickens's wholeheartedness is a significant connection of novelist and story, authorial energy and novel's worldview, because this book is so concerned with wholeness.

For Oliver food is always a primary matter, and his well-being is continually in question as he is struck, sickened, and even shot. Even though his "sturdy soul" may shine forth readily in his face to attract supportive friends, Oliver through much of the story struggles against the forces so determined to discredit him. More generally, the novel's oppositions of workhouse and family hearth, slum and country bower, present a fragmented world, a society very much in want of wholeness. Most of all, Dickens insists, this is a world in want of heart, but even among the best hearted, Brownlow and the Maylies, there is pain and separation, and we should remember that the principal villain, Monks, originates in the respectable world, not the underworld.

The novel's fable is one of progress toward wholeness, toward integrity of the self, and if this is possible for the title character, whom the law never recognizes as "legitimate," then there may be some prospect for more collective wholeness. So much for the fable that may serve as the moral and the end of the narration: the "truth" of *Oliver Twist*'s realism is that wholeness is a fable seldom attainable because it is easily corruptible, a once and future ideal.

Through their rationalizings, the "philosophic gentlemen" of the workhouse board see theirs as efforts benefiting the whole of society. From his underworld experience Fagin puts forth a strong case for the collective valuing of "number one," a case more tolerable when represented by the Artful Dodger and more ridiculous when epitomized by the rise and fall of Bumble the beadle. In depicting these viewpoints Dickens seems fascinated but somewhat uneasy in his comedy, and readers have often been puzzled about how to respond. Is his satire of the workhouse board a specific indictment of utilitarian political economy? How sympathetic is he to Fagin?

"Blackheartedness" typifies much of Dickens's imaginative intensity in *Oliver Twist*, for he seems most intense when writing about Fagin's London, Oliver's half-conscious fears, the murder of Nancy, and the last hours of Sikes and Fagin. Like Dostoyevski (who greatly admired his work) Dickens has an unflinching vision of human depravity; also like the Russian novelist he nonetheless maintains the expectation that however enfeebled, goodness will persevere. Although the persistence of goodness may be difficult to understand or explain, Dickens engaged himself whole heart and and soul with fictions he insisted were true, realistically describing the many evils and insisting on the progressive goodness of an Oliver.

6

"The Parish Boy's Progress"

Even without replicating the first readers' acquaintance with the serial that extended for more than two years, we find many reminders that this book was made up as it went along, and thus we may share the first readers' discovery that *Oliver Twist* is, as its subtitle suggests, "The Parish Boy's Progress" in more than one sense.

Dickens's subtitle plays on John Bunyan's *A Pilgrim's Progress*, and also it recalls the popular eighteenth-century caricature series by Hogarth, whom Dickens praises in his 1841 Preface to *Oliver Twist* as "the moralist and censor of his age—in whose great works the times in which he lived, and the characters of every time, will never cease to be reflected." In determining the *Oliver* subtitle, Dickens clearly had in mind Hogarth's *Harlot's Progress* and *Rake's Progress*. Bunyan's story, like Dickens's, was one of persistence, as the Christian made his harrowing way toward heaven, and as Janet Larson says, Dickens's allusions to Bunyan invite readers "to see behind the adventures of Oliver's story an archetypal struggle between the forces of good and evil for the hero's soul."[24] Hogarth's *Progress* drawings moved in the opposite direction of Bunyan's Puritan fable, for, like Dickens, Hogarth insisted on the "miserable reality" of London and presented criminals "in all the squalid misery of their lives; to show them as they really are, for ever skulking uneasily through the dirtiest paths of life, with the great black ghastly gallows closing up their prospect" (1841 Preface).

Dickens's and Hogarth's views of criminals as those consigned to a hell on earth with little or no prospect for redemption complement the Puritan view of the damned and the elect as they graphically update and particularize it for the eighteenth and nineteenth centuries. The notable difference between Hogarth's depictions of "progress" and Dickens's is that although the rake and harlot are on irreversible paths downward, Oliver holds true on the Bunyanesque course toward heaven.

Even if we do not recognize the Bunyan and Hogarth echoes, Dickens's subtitle suggests that all will be well, because in common usage, "progress" connotes "improvement." To English readers of the nineteenth century, however, the older sense of "progress" may have meant merely a movement from place to place (the travels of royalty from estate to estate had long been termed "royal progresses"), and such implications of the *Oliver Twist* subtitle undercut any promise it gives for its protagonist's ultimate happiness.

However closely we attend to the subtitle as descriptive and predictive of Oliver's circumstances, it reminds us this is a novel that is itself "progressing," literally from month to month; both Oliver and *Oliver Twist* are under way. As we read it today we can talk about the developing novel, mindful that, like "progress," the term "development" may promise more fulfillment than the serial composition and publication in fact delivered.

Those who come to this Dickens novel after reading some of his later work are likely to find the beginning strained and overstated, even for an author whose characteristic method was exaggeration. Compared with, say, the wonderfully immediate description of foggy London that opens *Bleak House*, *Oliver Twist* begins by distancing us from particulars:

> Among other public buildings in a certain town which for many reasons it will be prudent to refrain from mentioning, and to which I will assign no fictitious name, it boasts of one which is common to most towns, great or small, to wit, a workhouse; and in this workhouse was born, on a day and date which I need not take upon myself to repeat, . . . the item of mortality whose name is prefixed to the head of this chapter. (ch. 1)

Dickens's circumlocutions in the name of "prudence"—and in an apparent concern not to involve readers "at this stage of the busi-

ness at all events" in particulars that "can be of no possible consequence"—are familiar ploys of the realist. His is the method of the
book or film that, by insisting that "any resemblance to actual people or places is coincidental," suggests the fiction is so real that it
must pretend to be a fiction. The fiction of the fiction, then, is that
this is too true to be admitted as such.

In this opening, as so often happens when one uses literary
convention, Dickens is both imitative and innovative. He imitates
his favorite eighteenth-century novelists who would often use only
the initials for certain characters. Samuel Richardson's scoundrel
was "Mr. B___" in *Pamela*, parodied by Henry Fielding in *Shamela*
as "Booby." Tobias Smollett began *Roderick Random* with deliberate
obscurity of locale: "I was born in the northern part of this united
kingdom." Daniel Defoe's *Moll Flanders* started by stating the need
for not revealing the title character's real name—self-protection
similar to the "deep cover" our legal or espionage agencies occasionally provide. In refusing to give the place of Oliver's birth even a
fictional name, however, Dickens departs somewhat from literary
convention and probably has done so because he knows his readers may have been aware of real places represented by the fictional
place names in *Sketches by Boz* and his use of actual place names
in the then currently appearing *Pickwick Papers*. We know that his
first inclination had been to locate the *Oliver Twist* workhouse in
"Mudfog," the fictional town in which several of the *Sketches* had
been located, and in one of the subsequent months when he did
not publish a segment of *Oliver* he informed a friend that "the great
length of the proceedings of the Mudfog Association prevents the
insertion of the usual continuation this month" (*Letters*, 1: 301). By
not setting the workhouse in any of the fictional places to which he
had introduced readers in his other writing, Dickens furthers the
sense that this is an actual workhouse in an actual place and one
representative of any number of actual workhouses. Thus the *Oliver
Twist* workhouse is typical of a system rather than simply a particularly bad example.

For all Dickens's effort to establish the realism of his subject,
the opening sections of *Oliver Twist* seem highly artificial: the narrator's literary affectation undercuts the realistic conventions. Like
many writers with little experience, Dickens seems often to want to
convince us that he can sound like an author. The sentence struc-

tures of eighteenth- and nineteenth-century English novels (with few such relieving exceptions as Jane Austen) can try the patience of modern readers, and the sentences of Dickens's early novels seem often to exhibit the disintegration of periodic construction, witty playfulness, and even helpful punctuation that marked the best prose of the eighteenth century. Even if we account for the rambling nineteenth-century sentence as a style devised more for the ear than the eye, because so much fiction may have been written with the expectation it would be read aloud, the prose can be self-defeating.

As a stylist Dickens was both excessive and self-critical in his earliest fiction: both *Sketches* and *Pickwick Papers* are uneven, with concise and imaginative description and dialogue often appearing alongside writing so affected and turgid that we want either to despair or to believe that Dickens is switching to parody—maybe even of himself. Whatever his lapses, he occasionally becomes self-conscious enough to comment on his own excesses. In *Pickwick Papers*, for example, after describing a September morning as one on which "many a young partridge . . . strutted complacently among the stubble, with all the finicking coxcombry of youth," he stops with the realization, "But we grow affecting: let us proceed." He then begins a new paragraph with "In plain common-place matter-of-fact, then, it was a fine morning" (*PP*, ch. 19).[25]

Readers of the beginning of *Oliver Twist* may well wish it had more "common-place matter-of-fact" writing, for the opening pages continually remind us that this is the work of someone exuberantly practicing his art in ways that call for readers' patience. In the turnings and twistings of his indirection, Dickens at once informs readers that, had Oliver not survived his infancy, "these memoirs would never have appeared, or, if they had, being comprised within a couple of pages, that they would have possessed the inestimable merit of being the most concise and faithful specimen of biography extant in the literature of any age or country" (ch. 1). Coming as the intrusive voice of the satirist who hastens to assure us that he cannot regard birth in a workhouse as "the most fortunate and enviable circumstance that can possibly befall a human being," such labored prose does little to give readers access to Dickens's fictional world, and they may well wonder just what sort of author is begging their attention to his commentary.

Initially, then, even the forbearing reader experiences a version of the relationship the author himself has raised about his subject: Just what or where is the fiction? Is it "biographical memoir" or is it the author's commentary on the conditions and meanings of the life he has invented? Such questions engage the reader's imagination and, if dwelt upon, enforce the impression that there are similarities in the writing and reading processes. Even if this connection is more felt than understood, there is a bonus for the reader—an opportunity to participate imaginatively in the fiction. This is the magic that occurs when Dickens's fictional people and places come to life, spring forth preemptively in ways that let us forget that their existence is in any way contingent on the author or circumscribed by their functions in the story.

With more practice as novelist, Dickens subsequently achieved this effect more efficiently than he was able to in *Oliver Twist*, but even as the first monthly number concluded, the focus shifted from the narrator's circumlocutions to the immediacy of Oliver's first days. How much more directly the surgeon's instructions to give the child "a little gruel" but not to trouble him further characterize institutional indifference than do any of the narrator's literary affectations. And as the second chapter summarily traces Oliver's first nine years, Bumble the pompous beadle, through every self-promoting word and gesture, represents the workhouse more convincingly than any report or commentary by the narrator. As Bumble enacts Dickens's social commentary, he is one of those hypocrites who thrives on self-confidence, duplicitous to all but himself, and is therefore pathetically but particularly human. It is in Bumble's total comfort in his own perceptions and assertions that he is most like the novelist, and he delights in the ring of his rhetoric: "Mr Bumble had a great idea of his oratorical powers and his importance. He had displayed the one, and vindicated the other. He relaxed" (ch. 2).

The pattern of this first number (chapters 1 and 2) loosely governs the entire novel: the opening personifies the powers that oppose Oliver, predicts a dire future, and leaves his fate uncertain. After the famous encounter with the workhouse master when he dares to ask for "more," a gentleman in a white waistcoat says he is convinced "that boy will come to be hung." As the next installment begins we indeed find that for the past week "Oliver remained a close prisoner in the dark and solitary room to which he had been consigned by the wisdom and mercy of the board" (chs. 2 and 3). Oliver's early life is so uncertain that, huddled in this workhouse room, sleeplessly "drawing himself closer and closer to the wall, as if to feel even its cold hard surface were a protection in the gloom and loneliness which surrounded him," he crouches in the darkness to which Dickens later consigns Fagin.

The "progress" of many Dickens stories is punctuated by the wayside characters or events that enliven his fictional worlds, because in fiction, as in life, the incidental and unexpected so often claim notice. A case in point, among many in this novel, comes when Dickens mentions the poor donkey of the chimney sweep who wants Oliver as an apprentice. The donkey "was in a state or profound abstraction: wondering, probably, whether he was destined to be regaled with a cabbage-stalk or two," but instead it was beaten by its master (ch. 3). Without pausing to challenge the donkey's capacity for abstraction, we accept it as another resident of a hungering world, and quickly we find that its circumstances are precisely Oliver's, for both are underfed and abused. All this speaks forcefully without the narrator's gratuitous reminder that the gentleman in the white waistcoat takes the man's treatment of his donkey as proof he is "exactly the sort of master Oliver Twist wanted."

It is this eye for what another observer would consider dull and incidental that Dickens's readers come to enjoy and expect. His books, like his world, are crowded with people, places, and incidents that at first seem unconnected and eccentric, and his plots are often strained as they rationalize so many disparate elements, building toward endings that generally wrap together most of what has come before.

In *Sketches* Dickens had treated readers to many characters and scenes, remarking in "Thoughts about People": "It is strange with how little notice, good, bad, or indifferent, a man may live and die in London" ("Characters," ch. 1). As the roving reporter of *Sketches* Dickens gave notice to many obscure lives, but the point of this comment applies to what would be the central theme of his works—the need to recognize the interconnectedness of lives. Such later writings as *A Christmas Carol, Bleak House, A Tale of Two Cities,* and *Great Expectations* establish the ties of rich and poor, healthy and ill, past and present; as Scrooge's hard lesson teaches, to live fully is to live with sympathetic awareness. In Dickens's early writing such awareness is expressed largely through the narrator, for Boz is constantly present as the artist of *Sketches*. Too often at critical moments when readers need more direct expressions of Oliver's feelings and thoughts Dickens reverts to sketch writer and fails to attend closely enough to his character. For example, in chapter 10 when Oliver runs away from the bookstall where the Artful Dodger and Charley Bates had picked Mr. Brownlow's pocket, Dickens begins three successive paragraphs with people crying, "Stop thief! Stop thief!" and, as if pulling the camera back for the crowd scene as the music rises to the tempo of the chase, the novelist insists that "there is a magic in the sound" as "the cry is taken up by a hundred voices, and the crowd accumulate at every turning. Away they fly, splashing through the mud, and rattling along the pavements; up go the windows, out run the people, onward bear the mob; . . . and, joining the rushing throng, swell the shout, and lend fresh vigour to the cry, 'Stop thief! Stop thief!'"

Dickens's writing often reveals his fascination with mobs, but here to so turn from Oliver to the general subject of "a passion for hunting something [which is] deeply implanted in the human breast" (ch. 10) Dickens distracts attention from Oliver at a moment when the boy is confused and terrified. This early in the novel the reader—especially the reader who, through *Sketches* and *Pickwick*, had come to relish such Dickensian action scenes—may not object to the change of focus, but as the novel proceeds the difference between the all-seeing and frequently commenting narrator and the boy with such limited vision and expression becomes more troubling as "The Parish Boy's Progress" seems less important than is the narrator's getting on with his story.

The most abrupt shift of attention from title character to narrator comes at the opening of chapter 17 when Dickens stops to comment about storytelling, reminding readers of the custom "on the stage, in all good murderous melodramas, to present the tragic and the comic scenes, as in regular alternation, as the layers of red and white in a side of streaky bacon." Such interruptions of story were common in the eighteenth-century novel, and Dickens was not alone in using them in his own day. Although here he does not attempt to justify the commentary, it too belongs with literary artifices that "are not so unnatural as they would seem on first sight. The transitions in real life from well-spread boards to death-beds, and from mourning weeds to holiday garments, are not a whit less startling; only, there, we are busy actors, instead of passive lookers-on" (ch. 17). Dickens's task as storyteller is to achieve these transitions smoothly (a task greatly complicated by the improvisational demands of his serial writing), and he does so principally by being the most "busy actor" he can in the writing and by activating the readers' imaginations as well. The Dickens we hear in the passages just cited ("Stop thief!" and "good murderous melodramas") speaks to the passive reader, however, because the excited language he uses to describe the chase and his insistence on the underlying reality of melodrama intensifies rather than suspends the reader's sense that this is a play or a story.

There is less disjunction between the narrator-as-busy-actor and the reader-as-passive-onlooker because both narrator and reader become caught up in the novel's imagined lives. This process begins fairly early, for in contrast to the scene at the bookstall, where Dickens had shifted from Oliver's sense of things to the reader's view of the excited crowd, subsequent scenes have Dickens focusing better on even Oliver's vague sensations. When he is recaptured by Fagin and is about to be sent on a robbery with Sikes,

> Little Oliver's blood ran cold, as he listened to the Jew's words, and imperfectly comprehended the dark threats conveyed in them. That it was possible even for justice itself to confound the innocent with the guilty when they were in accidental companionship, he knew already. . . . As he glanced timidly up, and met the Jew's searching look, he felt that his pale face and trembling limbs were neither unnoticed nor unrelished by that wary old gentleman. (ch. 18)

Here it is Oliver who senses interconnection and complicity, and thus the relationship of actor and onlooker is a dynamic between him and Fagin, a tension the reader accepts as part of the story rather than commentary on it, even though the language is technically that of the omniscient narrator. The narrator is still very evident, because he is *telling* readers about Oliver, but he now is doing so in a way that keeps attention on what Oliver and Fagin are seeing and thinking rather than on what we or onlookers within the story may be seeing.

Twentieth-century readers may be overly fond of the storyteller who *shows* and not receptive enough to the more discursive nineteenth-century narrator we find in most of *Oliver Twist*. With the nearly two years he spent composing this novel and in his subsequent development of the "Sikes and Nancy" reading—in which he dramatized both the narrator's and characters' voices—we can see that, in his art, Dickens was proceeding toward more, not less, narrator involvement. The nature of this change is significant because his narrator grows less affected, less self-conscious in his satire and comments about the course of his story. He maintains a most sympathetic presence at such moments as the death of an old pauper woman (ch. 24) or Rose Maylie's life-threatening illness (ch. 29), or when recalling the gentle influence of peaceful country scenes that teach "us how to weave fresh garlands for the graves of those we loved" (ch. 32). Such sentimentality, while excessive to most readers, seems more in accord with the point of his novel than the stringent satire that so awkwardly punctuates earlier chapters. When confronted with the choice in his more mature novels, most Dickens readers would certainly prefer the satirical to the sentimental Dickens, but precisely because *Oliver* is a story of the progress from heartlessness to goodheartedness, from self-centeredness to a centering of the sturdy soul, the narrator's shift from a style marked most by satirical affectation to one prone to sentimental indulgence is appropriate thematically if not always satisfying esthetically.

These narrative extremes are ones we too readily may regard as gendered, with the satirical voice stereotypically that of male power and the sentimental that of female powerlessness. Such generalizations fail to account for the satirical genius of Jane Austen, Charlotte Brontë, or George Eliot, nor do they recognize the freedom a nineteenth-century male had in expressing feelings. The gender issue in *Oliver Twist* concerns the sources and centers of sympathies as well as the manner of expressing them. The book begins with the male author's view of a boy denied access to a very male-dominated world. Bumble's emblems of parochial authority are those of male power, complete with staff and semimilitary uniform, and male sexuality seems to lurk in his association of the pleasures of the flesh with his office. From his high-handed patronage of the baby farmer, the aptly named Mrs. Mann, to his calculating courtship of Mrs. Corney, Bumble is a sexually charged character, and one of the book's most apt jokes involves his loss of prowess when he is no longer a beadle.

In Oliver's early days at the workhouse and as an apprentice, he is in a world where women, like parish boys, have no station. The first deaths we hear of are those of Oliver's mother and of the pauper woman Sowerberry buries, and when we meet Oliver's friend Little Dick and learn of his vision of goodness and happiness, we find that he also is dying. The good and the beautiful and female are thus removed from the world of the Bumbles and Sowerberrys, and even when Oliver meets Nancy and Bet soon after he is introduced to Fagin he finds them untidy, stout, and hearty, with "a great deal of colour in their faces" and "remarkably free and agreeable in their manners" (ch. 9). This is as close as Dickens comes to calling them prostitutes, but the initial description places them readily in the gang where the kindly old gentleman is not truly kind. Much later Dickens insists that, although Nancy had squandered her life "in the streets, and among the most noisome [sic] of the stews and dens of London, . . . there was something of the woman's original nature left in her still" (ch. 40). This original nature was "the womanly feeling which she thought a weakness, but which alone connected her with that humanity, of which her wasting life had obliterated so many, many traces when a very child" (ch. 40). Because we see no such traces in the Nancy of earlier chapters, we may wonder whether this was a late idea of Dickens's as he moved toward the novel's climax, but the idea of womanly nature as threatened and often obliterated was evident throughout the story.

For Nancy in particular Dickens's letters indicate that by chapters 16 and 17 he hoped "to do great things with Nancy. If I can only work out the idea I have formed of her and of the female who is to contrast with her" (*Letters*, 1: 328). Rose, the other character he mentions, becomes the novel's principal locus of femininity, and Dickens's characterization of her was affected greatly by the death of his 17-year-old sister-in-law in May 1837. Mary Hogarth, who lived with the Dickenses, suddenly took ill and died unexpectedly in the novelist's arms. When, 10 days later, Dickens wrote to a friend to tell him of the loss, he found himself unable to "think and speak of her, calmly and dispassionately. I solemnly believe that so perfect a creature never breathed. I knew her inmost heart, and her real worth and value. She had not a fault" (*Letters*, 1: 259). Versions of Mary Hogarth appear in the majority of Dickens's books, but his grief over her death (which prohibited his writing an *Oliver Twist* installment for June 1837) clearly intensified his faith in female perfectibility at the very time he was writing a book in which his vision of male fallibility was so uncompromising.

Nancy, the fallen woman, finally dies as something of a martyr to a goodness that Oliver believes had died with his own mother (herself a fallen woman), and it is Nancy, therefore, who serves as one of the mother-sisters who sustain Oliver. Under Fagin's direction she poses as his sister to obtain information about Oliver's arrest, and she again assumes this part when Sikes recaptures Oliver in the street. But Nancy finds herself touched by Oliver in ways she cannot understand (perhaps because, via this book's symbolic logic, Oliver embodies virtue inherited from his mother—a virtue transmissible through him from woman to woman). After the recapture Nancy passionately protects Oliver against Fagin's and Sikes's violence, and they first think she is overplaying her part as "sister." Nancy, however, with words she repeats much later to Rose Maylie, acknowledges her own ruin but holds her own by threatening to expose the thieves if they harm Oliver. It is this threat, months later, that Fagin recalls when he lies to Bill Sikes and provokes him to murder Nancy. It is small wonder, then, that Bill's rage and subsequent torment are so intolerable, for they are perverse responses to generosity as much as they are acts of vengeance.

The life and death of Nancy counterpoint the parish boy's progress because her story demonstrates the terrible precariousness and vulnerability of humanity in the hands of brutes. If the novel had no Rose Maylie, no living female character to meet Nancy, to hear her story and mourn for her, there would be little credibility to Dickens's fable of persisting virtue. But Nancy's claim—a claim of womanly understanding on Rose—comes at the time when the story is also, and less convincingly, unraveling complications in Rose's own life: it is here we learn that she is Rose Fleming and thus Oliver's living female tie to his mother's family, as well as his link to Nancy.

The plot lines are difficult and probably unnecessary to remember, but the story logic is consistent with all that Dickens held important about Oliver himself: humanity will persist and good feelings survive and even prevail. Thus the "progress" that began so inauspiciously under the master of the workhouse ends with Oliver secure in the company of Rose, and the final illustration shows the two of them silent in front of the church memorial to Agnes Fleming, his mother.

This ending for "The Parish Boy's Progress" has transferred Oliver from parish workhouse to the parish sanctuary, from "ticketed item of mortality" (ch. 1) to adopted son of Brownlow, living "within a mile of the parsonage-house" of Rose and Henry Maylie, "linked together [in] a little society, whose condition approached as nearly to one of perfect happiness as can ever be known in this changing world" (ch. 53). Because Dickens made such a point of the mystery of Oliver's good nature and sturdy spirit, and because in the course of his story he made Oliver more often pawn than credible participant in his trials, these struggles do not seem explicitly those of manhood. Indeed, Oliver seems often to lack masculinity (early stage versions gave his part to actresses). The destroyed will of Oliver's father stipulated that if his illegitimate child were a girl, it was to have an inheritance unconditionally, but "if a boy, only on the stipulation that in his minority he should never have stained his name with any public act of dishonour, meanness, cowardice, or wrong" (ch. 52). We further learn that Oliver's father had taken these steps "to mark his confidence in the mother, and his conviction . . . that the child would share her gentle heart, and noble nature" (ch. 51). Thus it is the noble nature and gentle heart that the jealous, seizure-prone stepbrother so abhors, that the workhouse denies, and that Fagin and Sikes distrust, for all their versions of male authority depend entirely on their corrupting of Oliver and controlling of any women who possess gentleness or nobility of heart.

7

On the Face of It

> The dew seemed to sparkle more brightly on the green leaves; the
> air to rustle among them with a sweeter music; and the sky itself
> to look more blue and bright. Such is the influence which the
> condition of our own thoughts, exercises, even over the appear-
> ance of external objects. Men who look on nature, and their
> fellow-men, and cry that all is dark and gloomy, are in the right;
> but the sombre colours are reflections from their own jaundiced
> eyes and hearts. The real hues are delicate and need a clearer
> vision. (ch. 24)

Readers of *Oliver Twist* may not pay great attention to this brief
passage from chapter 24, but it can be a guide for understanding
Dickens's world view and art. It repeats the sentiments of his
farewell in *Pickwick Papers*, somewhat assuring readers that the
optimism with which he closed *Pickwick* had not been lost amid the
more harsh realism of *Oliver Twist*:

> Let us leave our old friend in one of those moments of unmixed
> happiness, of which, if we seek them, there are ever some, to
> cheer our transitory existence here. There are dark shadows on
> the earth, but its lights are stronger in the contrast. Some men,
> like bats or owls, have better eyes for the darkness than for the
> light. We, who have no such optical powers, are better pleased to
> take our last parting look at the visionary companions of many
> solitary hours, when the brief sunshine of the world is blazing full
> upon them. (*PP*, ch. 56)

Both passages insist on making, or making out, the best of a bright world, and although in both instances Dickens admits the existence of dark and evil, he closes *Pickwick* insisting on the inherent superiority of the light. Both passages emphasize the perceiver, and the one from *Oliver* qualifies idyllic description ("dew seemed to sparkle") and admits that for good or ill, "the condition of our own thoughts" influences the "appearance of external objects."

Thus the imaginations of Dickens and his characters may work as would that of Charlotte Brontë's Jane Eyre—to endow a scene with their own emotions. For the Victorian poets, especially, this would become the basic premise of the pathetic fallacy, but Jane Eyre's explicitness about the correlation of her human nature with a larger nature helps us understand Dickens's point about the face of nature reflecting our own faces. After the stormy night that follows Rochester's declaration of love to her, Jane awakens to sunshine and proclaims, "Nature must be gladsome when I was so happy."[26] The urgency of her "must" recalls Dickens's insistence that he has none of the owl's or bat's night vision and does not look on nature as the reflection of a jaundiced eye or heart. The early Dickens, then, like the yet-naive Jane, celebrates the powers of light, exercises them imaginatively with confidence in their inherent power and in his own imaginative power to maintain a clear vision.

On the face of it the world is bright and sunny, people are what they seem, and the positive influence of good thoughts may prevail. The characterization, plot, and contrasted settings of *Oliver Twist* seemingly separate its worlds into those of Fagin-Sikes-Monks and Brownlow-Maylie, claustrophobic workhouse and underworld set against expansive country life and well-kept townhouse. Oppositions of light and dark, tidiness and disorder, good and evil seem so obvious that Dickens's "real hues" may not appear to be at all "delicate" and may not seem to call for much "clearer vision." In the experiences of principal characters, however, this novel demonstrates that vision is often obscured, that people "look on nature, and their fellow-men, and cry that all is dark and gloomy."

Just as little Oliver's remarkable "sturdy" spirit constitutes the novel's romantic fable, its essential realism derives from Oliver's inability to win recognition and support as he moves from one to another of the contrasting worlds. Thus *Oliver Twist* is very much a story about those who face Oliver and how they cope with the challenges his very existence raises for them. To Bumble and Sowerberry he is but a commodity to be used to advantage; to Fagin and the boys he is a subject with whom to play and, as we later learn, to pervert; to Brownlow and Grimwig he is the incarnation of lost love, which they must nourish with some circumspection. To these characters Oliver is more important for what he represents than for what he does, and the omniscient narrator (and Dickens more directly in later prefaces) regards him as more emblematic than realistic—a demonstration of idealized life force, a reminder of humanity's need to connect not only with whatever friendly faces one can find in the course of one's life but with the numerous intimations of a transcendent past and future, a remembered childhood and a hope of heaven. The novel's opposing sets of forces have in common the desire to possess Oliver, and their ways of seeing him—most literally what they face with him—reveal their own varied conditions, their way stations on "The Parish Boy's Progress."

BUMBLE AND SOWERBERRY

We learn at once that, to the minds of the authorities, Oliver's status is clear once he is clothed, "badged and ticketed" (ch. 1). Bumble the beadle oversees the bringing up of Oliver "by hand" (a term at once suggesting the contradiction of deliberate care by bottle feeding and of having been beaten by harsh hands), naming him and speaking for him as long as he can. Bumble's colleague, the ironically named baby farmer Mrs. Mann, calls the beadle "quite a literary character" because of the various names he proposes for Oliver: "Twist" is preceded by "Swubble" and followed by "Unwin and Vilkins." In his earliest years Oliver is but an item, an "it," but just as he eventually shocks the system by asking for "more" he cries "lustily" as an infant. Such cries seem but the whimpers of an abused animal, and the association with animals recurs when he is nearly apprenticed to a chimney sweep, known for beating his donkey and therefore qualifying as "exactly the sort of master Oliver Twist wanted" (ch. 3). Spared this apprenticeship because a magistrate notes Oliver's "pale and terrified face," he finds himself fed the dog's food when he signed on with the undertaker, Sowerberry.

Sowerberry quickly capitalizes on Oliver's gaunt and melancholy experience and uses him as a child mute in funeral processions, a business innovation surpassing Mr. Sowerberry's "most sanguine hopes" (ch. 6). So draped, objectified, and silenced, Oliver, as a favorite of Sowerberry, is envied by the charity boy, Noah Claypool, and scorned by Mrs. Sowerberry. Oliver, as the narrator playfully puts it, "was not altogether as comfortable as the hungry pig was, when he was shut up, by mistake, in the grain department of a brewery." So too in the eye of the authoritative Bumble is Oliver's subsequent attack on Noah accountable in terms of diet, a "madness" resulting from the Sowerberrys' allowing him meat: "If you had kept this boy on gruel, ma'am, this would never have happened," says Bumble (ch. 7).

In this perverse society silence and starvation are both golden. To save food and treat the paupers poorly not only serves Bumble's greed, but, more broadly, the muteness of the hungry ensures their repression. Just as silence is the order for the poor, so ostentation is the mode for their masters. In the workhouse and in the apprenticeship, those in power establish their presence through speech and dress, through Bumble's official rhetoric and, with neat irony, down to the detail of his buttons bearing the parochial seal of the good Samaritan. Preying on starvation and sickness, the beadle and the undertaker lead comfortable, conscienceless lives, mimicking official concern for the welfare of young and old.

The opening seven chapters come across as broad, and sometimes heavy-handed, satire, but at several points Dickens demands that we more directly witness the most painful realities of pauperism. Most notably—perhaps because so well captured in the novel's first illustration—we see Oliver's and the other hungry boys' faces when he asks for more gruel. We hear that the bowls never needed washing because "the boys polished them with their spoons till they shone again," and in George Cruikshank's illustration their elongated heads, round eyes, and gaping mouths, make the boys themselves look like empty spoons and bowls. The master's first reaction to Oliver's rebellious request is to beat him with the empty ladle. We read of their hunger; we see at once their empty faces, reflecting graphically their scandalous diet.

"Oliver Asking for More." *George Cruikshank illustration.*

With the frequent help of illustrations, the text realistically depicts such scenes as the slum where Sowerberry and Oliver go to collect a pauper's body. With Oliver we find "the very rats, which here and there lay putrefying in its rottenness, were hideous with famine"—a condition Oliver realizes they share with the human residents. So as Dickens satirizes the self-servings of Bumble and Sowerberry and as he editorializes archly against the economic theories supporting the new poor law, his authorial descriptive eye is more incisive than those of the "authorities" he fictionalizes and criticizes. The overstatement here is one of heightened physical detail, documenting an urban scene teeming with corruption. Such descriptions work well, far better usually than the hyperbole of Dickens's more overt satire of parish officials.

THE ARTFUL DODGER

When Oliver attempts to speak out at the workhouse or undertaker's shop his comments are regarded as rebellious, criminal acts, and he provokes dire hints of the gallows as his destiny. The lively speech of the thieves he meets in his next stage seems to confirm this association of articulation and crime. Fagin revels in repartee with his boys, but above all the Artful Dodger epitomizes the liveliness of the unfettered word, holding its own until his eventual "sentencing" by the court. In appearance the Dodger is the reverse image of Sowerberry's carefully dressed mute, for he is a self-designed harlequin. "Snub-nosed, flat-browed, common-faced boy enough," he deliberately adopts "all the airs and manners of a man"—hat at rakish angle, oversized coat with rolled cuffs—and "altogether, as roystering and swaggering a young gentleman as ever stood four feet six" (ch. 8). His colorful and energetic speech, coded with the private vocabulary of thieves' cant, parallels the oddity of his appearance, but for all his swaggering self-importance he nonetheless assists Oliver in a way no one else ever has, for he buys him food and drink and offers shelter with his friend Fagin.

Never implicated in the darkest motives of the Monks-Fagin plot to discredit Oliver, the Dodger remains a Dickensian free spirit, a character sustaining himself through self-invention. Even though a scoundrel, he retains a kind of innocence through the resources of his own imagination. As James Kincaid has recognized, the Dodger's refusal to take "this monstrous society seriously is the best defense of the human spirit and the closest thing to a possible alternative to the system we have in this novel."[27] In this respect he is akin to Sam Weller of *Pickwick Papers*, Dick Swiveller of *The Old Curiosity Shop*, and the provincial theatrical company in *Nicholas Nickleby*. Within the darkest corners of this novel, the Dodger remains cheerful to the end, an exception to those whose "sombre colours are reflections from their own jaundiced eyes and hearts" (ch. 34). More clown than criminal, and although "one of the queerest-looking boys that Oliver had ever seen," the Dodger alone of the criminals has a familiar countenance and a persistently engaging manner.

In many respects the Artful Dodger is an alternate version of Oliver. Early on Bumble had wrongfully charged Oliver with being "artful" (ch. 3), but it is the Dodger who epitomizes the artfulness. Like the verbally resourceful Sam Weller of *Pickwick*, the Dodger reminds us that the art of language is often life's best dodge. Yet in his appearance as a child playing a man, the Dodger in some ways is antithetical to all Dickens holds sacred about childhood, for first and last Jack Dawkins is the articulate contrast to Oliver's often mute innocence. That he must play the part of boy-man and like Bumble construct a part for himself suggests that the child must, as Wordsworth put it, be a "little actor." But as his story shows, there remain important distinctions between the Dodger and the novel's other imposters; his survival seems to come at little or no cost to others, and his fate, therefore, will be transportation rather than confinement or execution.

Introduction of this talkative character complicates the narrator's own perspective, for as the Dodger talks his way into Oliver's qualified confidence the narrator looks over Oliver's shoulder to inform us that "Mr. Dawkins's appearance did not say a vast deal in favour of the comforts which his patron's interest obtained for those whom he took under his protection," and thus Oliver resolves that "if he found the Dodger incorrigible, as he more than half suspected he should, [he would] decline the honour of his farther acquaintance" (ch. 8). Like Dickens's other early novels *Oliver Twist* often fumbles with such strained language, and here we find the

narrator's observation empowering Oliver's mind with a self-awareness unlikely in a first encounter with a stranger. Although he is
likely to react with some caution given the way the aggressive Noah
Claypool treated him earlier, it is doubtful he could explain his
reactions in the way the narrator does for us. The affected narrative
tone parodies respectability and establishes the difference not simply between Oliver and the Dodger but between both of them and
the omniscient author. Yet a similarity remains between the
Dodger's and the author's stances, for both call attention to themselves through their language in ways that cause their audiences,
Oliver and readers, to marvel and perhaps to distrust their
verbosity.

The early chapters present many instances of language as
manipulative: Bumble "had a great idea of his oratorical powers
and his importance" in the bureaucracy; Sowerberry styled his
appearance and manner with funereal dignity. But the language
and performance of Fagin's gang impresses Oliver as spontaneous
and imaginative, for their life seems, under Fagin's feigned joviality,
but a game.

FAGIN AND THE BOYS

Nowhere in *Oliver Twist* is appearance more deceptive than in the
account of Oliver's introduction to Fagin and the boys. Although he
had reservations at once about the Dodger, he seems extraordinar-
ily slow to reach any understanding of the gang's objectives until he
is on the streets with them, even though he had been half-awake
enough to see and hear Fagin taking pleasure in his collection of
stolen goods and ruminating over the security of potential inform-
ers' having been hanged (ch. 9). Although we may wonder about
Oliver's persisting naïveté, this early interlude with the gang coun-
terpoints his earlier experiences in the workhouse and the apprenticeship. If the pauper's desire to possess even the resources to
survive may be criminal in the eyes of oppressive authority, then
such illegal possession as the gang has accomplished may indeed
be cause for celebration. To them, stealing is a contest, requiring

training and skill, and there is pleasure in the mere possession of property that is not immediately useful.

Fagin thus comes across as a hoarder, someone who enjoys having what he cannot use and has not yet disposed of for cash; he seems to have less desire to use or profit from his booty than simply to enjoy it. Long successful in his profession, he is pleased that "folks call me a miser, my dear—only a miser; that's all" (ch. 9). Much later as he faces imprisonment, Fagin will speak of the need to be at the top of his world, looking after number one so he can be number one, a principle applicable as well to Bumble and Sowerberry, were they to admit to principle. The charade of respectability that Oliver experiences is both true and false, true in the reality of the London underworld but false in Oliver's inability to recognize it as wrong. As the popular lyric from the musical *Oliver!* puts it, there may be great fun "picking a pocket or two" when in such convivial company.

The popular musical show of the 1960s and the Fagin show of the 1830s both conceal the real face of the criminal; in the words of Dickens's 1841 Preface, "the unattractive and repulsive truth" is present in neither. For readers, if not at once for Oliver, this truth becomes evident with the introductions of Fagin, Sikes, and Monks, all of whose faces, for what we see of them, are unattractive and repulsive. Fagin, with a "villainous-looking and repulsive face . . . obscured by a quantity of matted red hair," greets Oliver (ch. 8). Later Sikes specifically associates Fagin's with the devil's face: "There never was another man with such a face as yours, unless it was your father, and I suppose *he* is singeing his grizzled red beard by this time, unless you come straight from the old un without any father at all" (ch. 45). Similarly, Sikes has a "heavy, broad countenance," disguised by a three-day growth of beard and scowling eyes (ch. 13). But as the arch-villain, it is Oliver's half-brother, Monks, whose appearance is most ominous. Nancy says he has "eyes sunk in his head so much deeper than any other man's," a face "dark, like his hair and eyes," and lips "often discoloured and disfigured with the marks of teeth; for he has desperate fits, and sometimes even bites his hands and covers them with wounds" (ch. 46).

While we recognize in such descriptions the stereotypes of melodrama and sensational fiction, the anti-Semitism and crude pathology of crime in early Victorian England, these descriptions would be unworthy of attention were they not part of the novel's frequent attention to peoples' appearance and what can be read in any face. In Cruikshank's illustrations—as in our imaginations and surely in those of the many stage and film adapters of this novel—the criminals are obviously marked men. In the action of the novel, however, they take pains to conceal their appearances, working at night, lurking in hideaways; even Oliver, who has seen much of them, never succeeds in identifying any of them until Fagin already is in prison. At the center of the plot against Oliver is the half-brother who has operated under the assumed name of Monks, long lurking in pre-story past. To a novel so recollective of the past—be it in the form of lost childhood, the absent mother, a way of life seeming to antedate the world of urban crime—it is important to note that the residual evil, symbolized by Monks's hereditary disease and continuing jealousy, carries forward like the curse of Cain.

THE AMBIGUITIES OF GOODNESS

Stereotypes persist as the products of popular culture, but they point to long-prevailing assumptions about good and evil with the stereotypical villain appearing innately evil and irredeemable, capable only of becoming with each representation more hideous in act and visage. Such an assumption eliminates any need to complicate the problem of evil as the plight of the cosmologically "fallen" or of the economically doomed victims of capitalism, but the novel's presentation of "The Parish Boy's Progress" does raise what we can call problems of goodness, which Dickens addresses by insisting on the innate virtue of his hero, with a source or at least correlative in the natural world.

To this extent, Dickens writes in the tradition of William Wordsworth, and like fellow novelists Charlotte Brontë and George Eliot, he links the most positive human values with views of an emblematic natural world. In *Oliver Twist*, however, goodness is problematic because it survives where both heredity and environment would seem to rule it unlikely—Oliver is indeed illegitimate, "Work'us," as Noah Claypool taunts. This name-calling Oliver can bear, but Noah's attack on his mother's reputation causes Oliver to strike back; being a "natural" child, Oliver finds his very existence invaded by Noah's insult. Ultimately, Dickens insists on Oliver's unassailable innocence, evident in the boy's facial features, which must be taken as the token of his goodness.

Such an idealized presentation of Oliver can lead readers to mistake this as a novel of black and white, clearly distinguishing between the good that is in the heart (Oliver, after all, "possessed too much, rather than too little, feeling" [ch. 4]) and the evil manifest in the malice of criminal assaults on goodness. But when we look more closely at those who encounter Oliver and especially at their understandings both of him and the world, we find a much more problematic situation. As surely as the story insists on the persistence of Oliver's sturdy goodness (and, given his illnesses, is he really that sturdy?) so too does it recognize that his success is by no means guaranteed without some struggle. But the struggle is not in his soul where we would expect it; it occurs, rather, in the external world as Fagin attempts to poison his soul and as Brownlow seeks to find reason for supporting him. Eventually we learn from the story of Oliver's parents as well as from those of people he meets that the "cares, sorrows, hungerings of the world change faces as they change hearts" (ch. 24). Thus if goodness is so mutable, then there may be good reason for Fagin's thinking he has a chance of poisoning even Oliver's sturdy soul (ch. 19).

Although Oliver's benefactors generally respond positively to him, even they at critical moments have reason to distrust their impressions. In other words, what is at stake in this novel, as in many nineteenth-century stories, is the validity of values signaled, but not always manifest, in action and experience and correlated particularly by the beauty of the natural world. Thus a Jane Eyre insists readers join her in taking seriously "signs, sympathies, and presentiments" (ch. 21), Robert Browning's painter Fra Lippo Lippi must convince his superiors that the world "means intensely, and means good," and the grieving Lord Tennyson is comforted by the coming dawn at the climax of his spiritual searchings in *In Memoriam.* Such impulses toward a reaffirming nature pervade much of Dickens's writing, but even as early as *Oliver Twist* the reassurances of nature seem often faint and distant. As William T. Lankford argues, this source of "moral and metaphysical certainty" is no longer certain, for "no longer does visible nature provide a system of absolute correlatives to human feeling, and no longer does a character's appearance fully indicate his internal nature or his role in Providential design."[28] This is more true of the characters' failure to so find supportive evidence of goodness in the world and in one another than it is of the omniscient narrator's repeated insistence that, if seen rightly, Oliver's and nature's faces do carry affirmative messages. The novel is least convincing when this point is based solely on the perspective of the omniscient narrator and not on knowledge derived through the character's experiences. Such disparity between the characters' experiential knowledge and the narrator's optimism echoes the mixture of idealism and realism sounded in an 1834 pamphlet on the new poor law: the pamphleteer remarked that although "human nature must be acknowledged to be depraved, it still possesses sufficient integrity and intelligence . . . to pursue in general the . . . course of innocence, virtue, and industry" (*Times*, 2/8/1837).

It is not surprising for us to find something ghostly about Oliver, and he often serves as the reminder of a lost past as well as an example of present suffering. On at least three occasions—at Sowerberry's when empty coffins appear to take on human form, and twice when, half-asleep, he encounters Fagin—Oliver experiences the uncanniness of semiconsciousness. And to the half-brother to whom his presence is unbearable, he embodies an avenging spirit. But the most suggestive association of Oliver's countenance is its resemblance to his mother's portrait, its claim on Mr. Brownlow's memory, and its maintaining of the hope Oliver's dying friend, Little Dick, holds for heaven. For if, as little Dick expects, heaven is a congregation of happy faces, then the portrait of Oliver's dead mother (pictured within the Cruikshank illustration of Oliver comfortably situated in his earthly haven at Brownlow's) becomes an icon of a beatified spirit.

It is important to remember that Oliver neither looks at the portrait as a sort of mirror nor even yet realizes that this is his mother, although he feels an uncanny attraction to the image. At this point Oliver is recovering from a serious illness, and the Cruikshank illustration's relation of him to the portrait may serve as a subtle reminder of his survival as the persistence of his mother's goodness. Earlier associations of Oliver with death were more threatening, however. Dreadful as were his experiences in the workhouse and under Mrs. Mann, he is most terrified when, as the undertaker's apprentice, he goes to bed in the coffin workshop:

> An unfinished coffin on black trestles, which stood in the middle of the shop, looked so gloomy and deathlike that a cold tremble came over him, every time his eyes wandered in the direction of the dismal object: from which he almost expected to see some frightful form slowly rear its head, to drive him mad with terror. Against the wall, were ranged, in regular array, a long row of elm boards cut in the same shape: looking, in the dim light, like high-shouldered ghosts with their hands in their breeches-pockets. (ch. 5)

Corpses, coffins, and tombstones appear often in Dickens's novels, and the suggestion of ghosts with hands in their pockets anticipates the opening of *Great Expectations* when Pip gains from grave markers the uncanny impression that his five little dead brothers "had all been born on their backs with their hands in their trousers-pockets, and had never taken them out in this state of existence" (*GE*, ch. 1). The terror in *Great Expectations* comes not from death but from the convict Pip soon encounters. For Oliver, however, death is frightful in its nearness yet seems attractive as an alternative to his present suffering, and as he sleeps in "a recess beneath the counter" that "looked like a grave," he wishes "he could be lain in a calm and lasting sleep in the church-yard ground, with the tall grass waving gently above his head, and the sound of the old deep bell to soothe him in his sleep" (ch. 5).

The subsequent account of a pauper's burial, in "the obscure corner of the churchyard in which the nettles grew" and in a grave "so full, that the uppermost coffin was within a few feet of the surface," contrasts the reality of death with the idealizations of death that Oliver shares with Little Dick and that the novel seems to reiterate in its final homage to Oliver's dead mother (who, in fact, had died as obscurely as the shallowly buried pauper). Before he can be assured that death provides the opportunity for release from this life, Oliver needs to bring back to life as much of the idealized heaven that he can—a task requiring, as we shall see, the concomitant recapture of idealized childhood. Oliver's quest is partly a search for a place to live—a place where the peacefulness and beauty of the country churchyard are possible—and partly a search (in subtitle terms, a "progress") for recognition of his inherent worth, acknowledgment of his as a friendly face. So just as he is about to run away from Sowerberry, Oliver visits Little Dick, who describes his dream "of Heaven and Angels; and kind faces that I never see when I am awake" (ch. 7). The extent to which Oliver can find any heaven on earth depends on his finally locating kind faces and, correspondingly, being taken literally at "face value."

For this to occur Oliver must himself leave behind death wishes and shadowy impressions and begin to see the world as it is. His task is similar to those of David Copperfield and Pip, whose stories are more pointedly ones of developing self-awareness. Whereas David and Pip tell their own stories, Oliver is held more distant through omniscient narration, too often more seen than seeing, more the pawn of conflicting forces than the actor effecting or affected by change.

SLEEPING AND WAKING

Despite Oliver's prevailing passivity, however, we should pay close attention to the few instances when the novel focuses on his consciousness. In addition to the terrifying night among the coffins, there are two other occasions on which Oliver's view of the world is most uncertain. As he drowsily watches Fagin with his loot, Oliver finds himself in a state between waking and sleeping, which frees his mind "to form some glimmering conception of its mighty powers, its bounding from earth and spurning time and space, when freed from the restraint of its corporeal associate" 31 (ch. 9). Later, resting at Brownlow's and in a happier state, Oliver

> stirred, and smiled in his sleep, as though those marks of pity and compassion had awakened some pleasant dream of a love and affection he had never known; as a strain of gentle music, or the rippling of water in a silent place, or the odour of a flower, or even the mention of a familiar word, will sometimes call up sudden dim remembrances of scenes that never were, in this life; which vanish like a breath; and which some brief memory of a happier existence, long gone by; would seem to have awakened,

for no voluntary exertion of the mind can ever recall them.
(ch. 31)

This language repeats the imagery of Little Dick's earlier idealiza-
tion of death, and more directly echoes Dickens's response to a
reviewer's interest in his attention to Oliver's state of mind, claiming that passages such as this came "ready-made to the point of the
pen—and down it went."[29]

The novel's most sustained attention to the relationship of
dream and waking vision comes when Fagin and Monks peer in the
window of the country cottage where Oliver is asleep in a chair.
Here the narrator reminds us of the undoubted fact that, although
"our senses of touch and sight may be for the time dead, yet our
sleeping thoughts, and the visionary scenes that pass before us,
will be influenced, and materially influenced, by the *mere silent
presence* of some external object: which may not be near us when
we closed our eyes: and of whose vicinity we have had no waking
consciousness" (ch. 34).

The point of the incident intensifies the contiguity between the
novel's worlds, giving the criminal a simultaneous subconscious
presence in Oliver's dream and the countryside that seems so different from underworld London. Although no traces of them are
found after Oliver sees or thinks he sees them, there were other
reports of Monks's and Fagin's presence in the neighborhood.
Simultaneously for Oliver the real has been imagined and the
imagined has become real. Thus the character experiences briefly
what the reader may sense more broadly in a Dickens novel—the
proximity of the imagined to the actual.

Interestingly, the Cruikshank illustration shows Monks and
Fagin looking at the sleeping Oliver, who seems totally unaware of
their presence, and the choice of this as a subject for illustration
creates the impression that they actually were there, and we later
learn also that it had been necessary for Monks to assure himself of
Oliver's existence ("If you buried him fifty feet deep, and took me
across his grave, I should know, if there wasn't a mark above it,
that he lay buried there" [ch. 34]). The relative positions of object
and viewers in Fagin and Monks's encounter with Oliver at his window is reversed in the final installment's famous illustration of

"Monks and the Jew." *George Cruikshank illustration.*

Fagin in the condemned cell, where we, and Oliver, watch the felon in the condemned cell, where we, and Oliver, watch the felon huddling in terrified sleeplessness beneath the barred window. When we learn Fagin has sat, "awake, but dreaming," we find he has, in a sense, changed places with the Oliver of the earlier illustration. To be so seen and known is the only possible termination for the man who had so long been an elusive and shadowy figure, and the face once obscured is now wide-eyed with terror.

Through text and illustration, it is the confined Fagin we leave, not a Fagin at the gallows, for the book never describes his hanging. The penultimate chapter concludes with a reported public-execution scene wherein "everything told of life and animation" but where, conversely, there was a "dark cluster of objects in the centre of all—the black stage, the cross-beam, the rope, and all the hideous apparatus of death" (ch. 52). For a novelist prone to over-writing and sensationalizing, Dickens achieves a very powerful end by not showing Fagin's appearance on this final stage. The logic of his plot keeps Fagin private even in death, leaving in our view and in Oliver's a terrified prisoner rather than a public execution (a contemporary practice Dickens opposed).

The illustrations (often missing from paperback editions) are helpful in our reading of *Oliver Twist*, and the story itself takes portraiture seriously. As with the sometimes stereotyped and exaggerated appearances of the criminals, readers may regard the use of the picture of Oliver's mother as a mere prop, a popular writer's creaky plot machinery, but however much Dickens strains credibility by the string of coincidences that brings Oliver to the very room where his mother's portrait hangs, the idea of a face bearing association with fond memories and of a picture itself as an emblem of fine character was a familiar idea for nineteenth-century readers. Portraits and sketches, miniatures (and within a few years, daguerreotypes and photographs) were common, and the idea that character could shine forth from them certainly led many writers to create literary characters as though they were painting portraits. Most insistently, Thomas Carlyle would "read" the character of heroes from portraits of such people as Oliver Cromwell, and in his pen portrait of a man he had known, he recalled his friend's as "such a face as you would still more rarely see, . . . brow, cheeks, jaws, chin all betokening impetuosity, rapidity, delicacy, and the stormy fire of genius not yet hidden under the ashes of old age."[30] Granted, no such vivid detail distinguishes the portrait of the dead mother in Dickens's novel, but as did Carlyle, Dickens obviously put great stock in the reading of character through appearance.

BROWNLOW

Both Oliver, then, and those who assist him are struck immediately by something they do not understand in a face. For Oliver it is the woman's portrait that captures his attention, and Mr. Brownlow finds "something in that boy's face . . . that touches and interests me. *Can* he be innocent? . . . Where have I seen something like that look before?" (ch. 11). He sorts through his recollection of faces, many of which "the grave had changed and closed upon, but which the mind, superior to its power, still dressed in their old freshness and beauty." Here, in conscious remembering, is a way to bring Little Dick's notion of heaven and angels to life. When Brownlow sorts through his recollections, however, he cautions himself that his attraction to Oliver "must be imagination"—but this is precisely the point. As so often happens in the Dickens world, memory and imagination together call for faith and trust as surely as does Oliver's innocent face, but Brownlow proceeds cautiously. Brownlow's gruff associate, Mr. Grimwig, more impulsively insists Oliver must be a fraud, even though "in the inmost recesses of his own heart, Mr. Grimwig was strongly disposed to admit that Oliver's appearance and manner were unusually prepossessing" (ch. 14).

When recovering from illness after first coming to Brownlow's house, Oliver speaks of having dreamed of his dead mother, whose "face has always looked sweet and happy," and as he looks at the picture he remarks, "What a beautiful, mild face that lady's is!" Brownlow acknowledges that the boy is the picture's "living copy" (ch. 12). "Too much," we too readily mutter in annoyance at such contrived storytelling, but before dismissing the scene as clumsy, immature writing we should note that, as often when he seems to lapse, Dickens here recovers brilliantly. The revelation does not proceed to full explanation of the picture to Oliver or of Oliver to Brownlow, but instead the benefactor grows wary of what can only

"Oliver Recovering from the Fever." *George Cruikshank illustration.*

further his fear that he is imagining connection where none may exist. Soon Brownlow orders removal of the picture, ostensibly because it might upset Oliver unnecessarily but more likely because he must have more direct proof of Oliver's character and does not in the meantime want his imagination to be teased further. Brownlow claims that although he has been deceived before, affliction has strengthened and refined his best affections. Although he wants to trust in Oliver, he cannot fully rely on his sense that Oliver embodies the portrait's goodness, that the boy's is a face to join the crowd of those Brownlow fondly recalls.

Deception, betrayal of or by loved ones, is at the center of several lives in *Oliver Twist*, and there is no explanation of why passion can be so destructive for some and so ennobling for others. Monks felt himself and his mother betrayed by his and Oliver's father, and Brownlow characterizes Monks as someone "who from your cradle were gall and bitterness to your own father's heart, and in whom all evil passions, vice and profligacy, festered, till they found a vent in a hideous disease which has made your face an index even to your mind" (ch. 49). This is the condition Brownlow has rather remarkably avoided, for as the benefactor and family friend who twice restores Oliver, Brownlow, as Joseph M. Duffy has remarked, is not "an ineffectual patriarch" but "a man of organized experience who reacts in a vigorous personal manner to any affront to human order he encounters."[31] Were Brownlow to assume responsibility for telling the story of Oliver, he would tell it with a mixture of Oliver's naïveté, idealism, and trust, and even with some of Grimwig's not entirely comic cynicism. As the person who travels to the West Indies for information about Monks and who interrogates the Bumbles about the circumstances of Oliver's birth and about their collusion with Monks to destroy evidence of the parish boy's past, Brownlow becomes an "author" of the story: he makes the connections and forces the confession necessary to resolve the plot. Confronting Monks with knowledge of his villainy, Brownlow declares his to be "a true tale of grief and trial, and sorrow. . . . [S]uch tales usually are" (ch. 49).

Brownlow is the detective-author; his role, and his greatest success, becomes the proving of his initial assumptions about Oliver's and the portrait's correspondent virtues. Once more Dickens upsets his readers' anticipations, for we might well expect

Oliver's birth to have been proven legitimate because of a secret marriage. Such is not the case, however: it remains more important that Oliver be fully accepted *as* illegitimate and, in a more profound sense than Bumble's view of the law as "an ass," that there be a final approval of human love incomprehensible to corrupt institutions. Certainly, as Steven Marcus has said, vindication of Oliver's "illegitimacy is the event toward which the entire novel has been directed," a justification for Dickens in particular but for many of the nineteenth century's declassed and disinherited, of the outsider's rise to the station of "gentleman" (1968, 87).

THE "FALLEN WOMAN" AND IDEALIZED WOMANHOOD

The "outsider" most clearly given "station" in this novel other than Oliver himself is his deceased mother. We see her represented first in the recollections of those at the workhouse who saw her as yet another incarnation of the "old story" of the fallen woman, a version of which Oliver instinctively denies when he attacks Noah to defend her name. Then, as we have seen, she is represented by the portrait at Brownlow's. Finally, in the novel's last illustration, her name is inscribed on a memorial tablet "within the altar of the old village church." Just as in the Brownlow parlor illustration where characters looked at her portrait behind the seated Oliver, so here Oliver and Rose direct their eyes to the tablet. Interestingly, we can find some similarities between this illustration and that of Fagin in the condemned cell (which also appeared in the final installment). Both are darkened scenes, stone corners with a small window in the upper center, a bench against the wall; instead of the horrifics of cell bars, sheriff's orders on the wall, and a terrified convict on the bench, however, we have only the small latticed window, the tablet with Agnes's name, and the empty bench. This memorial-without-tomb conveys a discernible immortality in contrast to the condemned cell's signs of hideous mortality.

The iconography of the illustrations together with what the text establishes about Oliver's mother gives this unfortunate woman a posthumous home, and even a sort of sanctification. More broadly, in the novel's view of human potential fallen women present a particularly problematic case. Ultimately memorialized by church tablet and remembered as pictured and immortalized in her son and surviving sister, Rose, Oliver's mother's fate is the happy opposite to Nancy's. Yet it is the story of Nancy on which Dickens seems to center more of his imaginative interest. There are definite parallels in the stories of Nancy and the mother, Agnes, because of the common interests they have in Oliver and their common plight as "fallen women." The difference, of course, is that Nancy lives a life she has chosen and that ends with her murder. Agnes, on the other hand, was, we are told, the innocent victim of circumstance that precluded marriage with Oliver's father.

There has been considerable critical interest in Nancy as one of Victorian fiction's representations of a prostitute, and although Dickens was charged from the first with giving her inappropriately fine language, he vigorously defended the truthfulness of his characterization:

> It is useless to discuss whether the conduct and character of the girl seems natural or unnatural, probable or improbable, right or wrong. IT IS TRUE. . . . It is emphatically God's truth, for it is the truth He leaves in such depraved and miserable breasts; the hope yet lingering behind; the last fair drop of water at the bottom of the dried-up weed-choked well. It involves the best and worst shades of our common nature; most of its ugliest hues, and something of its most beautiful; it is a contradiction, an anomaly, an apparent impossibility, but it is a truth. I am glad to have had it doubted, or in that circumstance I find a sufficient assurance that it needed to be told. (1841 Preface)

As in his characterization of Sikes and the boys, Dickens is reporting the contemporary scene. The 1839 Constabulary Commission Report mentions burglars having their women as confidantes who, when drunk, often unwittingly betrayed the burglars by boasting of their prowess. So there was ample reason for Sikes to fear betrayal by Nancy, even had her meeting with Rose Maylie not been overheard by Noah Claypool.

It is not Nancy's mere presence but her relationships to other characters that attracts readers' attention. Despite her refusal to take full advantage of Rose Maylie's offers of help, she and Rose have strong interest in one another, springing perhaps from Rose's realization that, but for the good fortune of a supportive foster family, Nancy's could have been her fate. In terms similar to Dickens's in defense of Nancy, Rose comprehends that although Nancy's life was "squandered in the streets, and among the most noisome [*sic*] of the stews and dens of London, . . . there was something of the woman's original nature left in her still" (ch. 40). Qualities so stereotyped and valorized as feminine link Nancy's better nature to both Rose and Agnes Fleming, whose portrait bore such signs long after her death. Here too we find a consistency in the novel's view of the present world as containing intimations of some better time, reminders surviving in some human faces and on the face of nature, and there is a generalized Christian consolation in the expectation that through death the lost world becomes more accessible. When the old pauper, Sally, dies, the narrator's comment expands Little Dick's earlier notion of heaven as acquaintance with friendly faces:

> Alas! how few of Nature's faces are left to gladden us with their beauty! The cares, and sorrows, and hungerings, of the world, change them, as they change hearts; and it only when those passions sleep, and have lost their hold forever, that the troubled clouds pass off, and leave Heaven's surface clear. It is a common thing for the countenances of the dead, even in that fixed and rigid state, to subside into the long-forgotten expression of sleeping infancy, and settle the very look of early life; so calm, so peaceful do they grow again, that those who knew them in their happy childhood, kneel by the coffin's side in awe, and see the Angel even upon earth. (ch. 24)

The association of childhood innocence with reassurances of blissful immortality had particular urgency for Dickens at this time of his life, because the year before he had lost Mary Hogarth, his beloved 17-year-old sister-in-law. He described her as having had "abilities far beyond her years, with every attraction of youth and beauty, and conscious as she must have been of everybody's admiration, she had not a single fault" (*Letters*, 1: 263). With such a viewpoint, substantiated further by recollections of his own as such a special but by no means innocent childhood, Dickens would go on to idealize, and in various ways immortalize, childhood. In his later novels children reverse roles with their elders, demonstrate preternatural wisdom, and remain well attuned to the signs of transcendent beauty and hope. Thus in *The Old Curiosity Shop* Little Nell, the most famous example of a dying child in nineteenth-century literature, finds consolation among the memorials of an old country church. Smike, liberated in *Nicholas Nickleby* from a dreadful boarding school, finds peace in a country garden before he too dies. With these and such other fictional children as the little but oddly old-looking Paul Dombey, Dickens secularizes the scriptural admonition "except as a little child" and admits to his fiction a fact of nineteenth-century life—its high rate of infant and childhood mortality. Even the corpse of James Steerforth, the betrayer and seducer in *David Copperfield*, suggests this possibility to David, who recognizes a resemblance between the dead body and the memory he has of Steerforth sleeping peacefully as a schoolboy. It is precisely because Sikes murders Nancy by brutally bashing her face, disfiguring her so badly, that this murder is so horrible. Whatever vestiges of idealized womanhood had remained in her face are now unrecognizable, yet her eyes continue to enflame Bill's mind during his mad flight from the scene of the crime. Given the idealizations of peaceful death both in this novel and more generally in Dickens, it is not surprising that the murder of Nancy became the subject of Dickens's most frightful and most favorite reading, "of all bad deeds that, under cover of the darkness had been committed within wide London's bounds since night hung over it, that was the worst. Of all the horrors that rose with an ill scent upon the morning air, that was the foulest and most cruel" (ch. 48). What makes this crime so exceptional is its violation of the most sacred center of humanity in the imaginative world of *Oliver Twist*. It is not simply a matter of obliterating the remnants of womanly goodness or even of the brutality of undeserved punishment. Rather, Nancy becomes the victim of Bill Sikes's, and by association the underworld's, unmitigated rage against innocent goodness, in kind not unlike Noah Claypool's early attack on young Oliver or Monks's determination to obliterate all documents that would identify him. The most telling detail of the murder is that it is Nancy's face turned up to his own that Bill pistol-whips "with all the force he could summon" (ch. 48). In a novel where heaven and a better life on earth is expressed in terms of happy faces, this disfigurement is an attack on the life force itself.

Sikes's principal motive for the murder is that Nancy had spied on and betrayed his associates, and thus it becomes impossible for Bill to rid himself of the specter of Nancy's eyes as he tries to evade arrest. Dickens well describes a psychology of guilt, and it is a guilt not simply for this act but for an attack on humanity itself:

> For now, a vision came before him, as constant and more terrible than that from which he had escaped [the sight of Nancy's body]. Those widely staring eyes, so lustreless and glassy, that he had better borne to see them than to think upon them, appeared in the midst of the darkness: light in themselves, but giving light to nothing. (ch. 48)

Previously, Sikes had been a creature of the darkness, and now he has the sense of disembodied eyes pursuing him, as uncompromising light possesses him. Immediately after killing Nancy he finds bright sun breaking into the room: "He tried to shut it out, but it would stream in. If the sight had been a ghastly one in the dull morning, what was it, now, in all that brilliant light!" (ch. 48). Dickens's prompt copy for the reading version here contains the marginal notes (all twice underlined) "Action," "Mystery," and "Terror to the End" (*SN*, 39). The terror, then, is of seeing as well as being seen. Before he dies Sikes tries desperately to flee back into the night at Jacob's Island, "the filthiest, the strangest, the most extraordinary of the many localities that are hidden in London." Yet here too he is pursued and watched as he accidentally hangs himself while trying again to flee (ch. 50).

Similarly, Fagin's trial brings exposure. At his sentencing we share his surrealistic sense of the court

> filled from floor to roof, with human faces. Inquisitive and eager eyes peered from every inch of space. From the rail before the dock, away into the sharpest angle of the smallest corner in the galleries, all looks were fixed upon one man—the Jew. Before him and behind: above, below, on the right and on the left: he seemed to stand surrounded by a firmament, all bright with gleaming eyes. (ch. 52)

Fagin earlier feared that the waking Oliver may have watched him enjoying his hoard, so now confrontation with such a "firmament" must utterly unnerve him. It is at this point of conclusion that the novel's public and private worlds separate, for, as we have seen in text and illustration, Fagin's last hours are private ones for us and Oliver to witness, and what comfort and restoration may be possible are most evident within the small circle that forms to honor Agnes and her son.

This ending of *Oliver Twist*, like those of many Dickens novels, may seem more restorative, even retrogressive, than realistic, for like the ending of a romance it detects and corrects past injustices, rewards the persevering and punishes the evil-doers. The right people, Henry and Rose, are free to marry, and Oliver has a home. In general the ending is entirely conventional, and as the narrator takes leave of his characters (and readers) he wishes to "linger yet with a few of those among whom I have so longed moved, and share their happiness by endeavouring to depict it" (ch. 53). He realizes his to have been the role of watcher and portrait painter, and, appropriately, it is as such a recollector that he describes himself, wishing he could "summon before me once again, those joyous little faces that clustered round [Rose's] knee. . . . These, and a thousand looks and smiles, and turns of thought and speech—I would fain recall them every one" (ch. 53).

Thus, although the future may be uncertain beyond his predictions of bliss for the wedded and worthy, the novelist has re-created a secure past. So too has Oliver, literally returning to his past, found instant assurance in the visible world—"That's the stile," and so forth. Such self-verification was often impossible earlier, when people seemed to disappear and addresses to change before his eyes. But now, in the fiction of recollection, Oliver, like Scrooge as guest of the first spirit, delights in visions of his lost childhood. For Oliver this is the opportunity to revel in a final view of "pure, earnest, joyful reality" (ch. 51). Despite a sentimental conclusion assuring continued domestic happiness for the Maylies, it is the manner more than the matter of Dickens's ending that definitively connects his concept of novel writing (and, by implication, novel reading) with the story's constant attention to what people see and "read" in city and country scenes and, most particularly, in expressive faces.

8

Fagin

Although not the principal villain and, in fact, like Oliver a victim of both social institutions and the evil Monks, Fagin is the center of much of the novel's imaginative and emotional energy. He is one of those Dickens creations that remains with readers long after they forget much else in the story. He represents an idea and seems often to be Dickens himself enacting a sort of authorship as he shapes his little world. Caught up in the writing, Dickens, who did the most of his work in the morning, told a friend that he "had great difficulty in keeping hands off Fagin and the rest of them in the evenings" (*Letters*, 1: 328). To Oliver, Fagin is both fearsome and fascinating, and, as does Oliver, readers well may wonder what to make of him. Coming, as we shall see, from a variety of sources, Fagin is a composite of Dickens's personal hauntings, of criminals who skulked his London, and of other figures from literature.

Dickens's illustrator, George Cruikshank, took particular interest in drawing this character, keeping him literally before readers' eyes as a Cruikshank as well as a Dickens creation. Soon after Dickens's death, Cruikshank claimed that he had been responsible for Dickens's casting of a Jew as a fence, but this has not been substantiated. Curiously, however, the Fagin illustrations closely resemble a self-portrait Cruikshank earlier made for one of the *Sketches by Boz*, where he had included both himself and Dickens, and in later life Cruikshank would sit in front of a mirror to assume the terrifying pose of Fagin in the condemned cell.[32]

Throughout his long career Cruikshank often represented himself as frightening, with long black hair, glaring eyes, and a large nose. Just as Dickens, when nearly finished with his novel, would speak to a friend of Fagin as "such an out and outer that I don't know what to make of him" (*Letters*, 1: 441), Cruikshank in later years regarded his public appearances in a similar way: in an 1841 *Omnibus* cartoon he showed himself shocking a drawing-room group.[33] Dickens's and Cruikshank's coincident personal interest in Fagin was manifested in their powerful combination of text and illustration, and the fascination novelist and illustrator had with this creation was well recognized by G. K. Chesterton, who more frequently celebrated the cheerfully comic Dickens:

> In the doubled-up figure and frightful eyes of Fagin in the condemned cell there is not only a baseness of subject; there is a kind of baseness in the very technique of it. It is not drawn with the free lines of a free man; it has the half-witted secrecies of a hunted thief. It does not look merely like a picture of Fagin; it looks like a picture by Fagin.[34]

Fagin's origins are multiple, but surely the most pronounced root leads to Dickens's boyhood, as revealed in a fragmentary autobiography he entrusted to his friend and biographer, John Forster. So many of Dickens's anxieties and so much of his determination to succeed derive from experiences during the short period when, as a boy of 12, he was sent to work pasting labels at Warren's Blacking Warehouse. As this autobiographical sketch describes Warren's, Dickens might as well have been working in the *Oliver Twist* underworld:

> The blacking-warehouse was the last house on the left-hand side of the way, at old Hungerford Stairs. It was a crazy, tumble-down old house, abutting of course on the river, and literally overrun with rats. Its wainscoted rooms, and its rotten floors and staircase; and the old gray rats swarming down in the cellars, and the sound of their squeaking and scuffling coming up the stairs at all times, and the dirt and decay of the place, rise up visibly before me, as if I were there again. (Forster, 1: 23)

By the time Dickens wrote this in the mid-1840s he had, figuratively, been there repeatedly by writing about such places, especially in *Oliver Twist*, *The Old Curiosity Shop*, and *Martin Chuzzlewit*, but his recollection had associated *Oliver*, especially, with this time and place. For all the squalor of the workhouse and of the slum he had visited with Mr. Sowerberry, Oliver finds Fagin's den the most wretched place he has seen. Held there against his will, he finds himself in surroundings remarkably similar to those Dickens recalled from the blacking warehouse:

> It was a very dirty place. The rooms upstairs had great high wooden chimney-pieces and large doors, with panelled walls and cornices to the ceilings. . . . Spiders had built their webs in the angles of the walls and ceilings; and sometimes, when Oliver walked softly into a room, the mice would scamper across the floor, and run back terrified to their holes. (ch. 18)

Dickens's later acknowledgment of the warehouse days as the source for Fagin's name firmly links *Oliver*'s criminal world with the past Dickens so long concealed even from his family. Dickens's autobiographical fragment recalls the boys among whom he had been cast:

> Two or three other boys were kept at similar duties down-stairs on similar wages. One of them came up, in a ragged apron and paper cap, on the first Monday morning, to show me the trick of using the string and tying the knot [on blacking bottles]. His name was Bob Fagin; and I took the liberty of using his name, long afterwards, in *Oliver Twist*. (Forster, 1: 51, 52)

Because the warehouse episode was such a source of shame for Dickens and such a forceful reminder of how a working-class life was just a step away from the workhouse if not prison (this was the time his father was in debtor's prison), he confesses being more ashamed than grateful for Bob Fagin's kindnesses: "No words can express the secret agony of my soul as I sunk into this companionship; compared these every-day associates with those of my happier childhood; and felt my early hopes of growing up to be a learned and distinguished man, crushed in my breast" (Forster, 1: 53).

We can see, then, how much of Dickens's most secret past resides in the name Fagin. The novel's Fagin, like Dickens's warehouse colleague, instructs; rather than teaching the tricks of such honest employment as bottle-wrapping, however, he is master in training boys the trickery of picking pockets. Fagin, a secretive character, living in places resembling Dickens's recollections of the warehouse and exercising power over boys, is in part a belated scapegoat for Dickens's secret agony. John Bayley well describes the transformation of the kindly boy, Bob Fagin, into the Fagin of *Oliver Twist*:

> So passionate was the young Dickens's desire for the station in life to which he felt entitled, and so terrifying his sense that it was being denied him, that he must have hated the real Fagin for the virtue he could not bear to accept or recognize in that nightmare world, because it might help to subdue him into it. The real Fagin's kindness becomes the criminal Fagin's villainy.[35]

Certainly the autobiographical fragment invites this sort of speculation, but to recognize likely motives for Dickens's use of the Fagin name, and for situating him as a criminal, we need to understand the imagination both behind and within this character. The Fagin we meet in the novel is a concentration of Dickens's resentment over having to work in the warehouse; Fagin's is a dynamic, imaginative presence that fascinates his creators—Dickens and subsequently Cruikshank. Although he incorporates many of the stock features of the criminal, the outcast Jew, and even the devil, his impact on both Oliver and the novel's various worlds is sufficient to alert readers to a depth and power we would not ordinarily expect from such a character. Even the most cursory comparison with Dickens's handling of Bumble as a comic caricature or, on the other hand, of Monks as a demon, indicates the far more complex nature of the Fagin characterization.

As we can see from the ways adapters, beginning with Cruikshank and continuing to the twentieth century with the musical *Oliver!*, have represented him (in *Oliver!* he is a comic lead), Fagin is the character on whom the story's importance hinges, and he is one readers appropriate according to the seriousness with which they take Dickens's novel. Whatever he is, however fully he incorporates the novelist's vision of childhood suffering, a contemporary underworld, and an idea of evil that somehow must be confined, Fagin remains the novel's most intriguing character precisely because we can never be certain just who he is or what he really represents. As

Robert Tracy points out, Oliver separated from Fagin's creative energy "loses whatever animation he has possessed."[36]

As with many of Dickens's most memorable characters, Fagin teases us into reading Dickens himself in the characterization. It is most tempting to consider Fagin a sort of author, for like the novelist he orchestrates the actions of his subordinates, reveals and conceals character, and has a plan for the life around and ahead of him. Furthermore, he is quite an actor, performing his own scripts; he is, briefly, a philosopher, accounting for himself with a world-view that upholds the individual. Within the novel's different worlds there are self-interests that confine and separate individuals, be they members of Fagin's gang, Brownlow's circle, or the Maylie family. John Bayley believes that this process thematically unifies the novel: "Normal living and the life of crime are almost indistinguishable in *Oliver Twist*, for both are based on the burrow" (1962, 451).

Whatever the shame or guilt or self-justification or vision of society Dickens worked through in portraying Fagin, this character possesses an identity far removed from the blacking warehouse. The novel's first readers probably had no sense of any of Dickens's personal history lurking in Fagin but could associate him with Jews and criminals from real life and fiction. Readers sensitive to young Oliver's view of Fagin might even hear echoes of fairy tale, especially when this wolfish man greets the boy with "Delighted to see you looking so well, my dear" (ch. 16).

Although literature presented Dickens with a long tradition of villainous Jews from which to draw, he claimed to have sketched Fagin from life. In his 1841 Preface he wrote, "It was, it seemed, a coarse and shocking circumstance, that some of the characters in these pages are chosen from the most criminal and degraded in London's population: that Sikes is a thief and Fagin a receiver of stolen goods; that the boys are pickpockets, and the girl is a prostitute." His defense of Fagin as an accurate portrayal is corroborated by the Metropolitan Police's constabulary commission, which in 1839 declared that, for the most part, fences were all Jews. There has been an inconclusive but long-running argument over particular Jews as prototypes for Fagin. Anti-Semitism in Fagin's characterization did not provoke the outrage we might expect for at least two decades following the novel's 1837 publication. England's

Jews gained rights and respectability very slowly through the mid-nineteenth century, and even by 1850 there were only about 30,000 Jews in Britain. In 1861 journalist Henry Mayhew commented that popular feeling had run against Jews since the eighteenth century:

> They were considered—and with that exaggeration of belief dear to any ignorant community—as an entire people of misers, usurers, extortioners, receivers of stolen goods, cheats, brothel-keepers. ... That there was too much foundation for many of these accusations, and still *is*, no reasonable Jew can now deny; that the wholesale prejudice against them was absurd, is equally indisputable. (Mayhew, 3: 117)

It was this kind of wholesale prejudice in his characterization of Fagin that Dickens later found himself called to account for. In 1860 Eliza Davis, the wife of the Jewish banker who had bought the novelist's former home, wrote to Dickens seeking his help for a Jewish charity and complaining about the injustice of his portrayal of Fagin. Dickens replied by repeating his earlier claim that he had simply been realistic; fences invariably had been Jews at the time he had written the novel. Mrs. Davis persisted by pointing out to Dickens that an author of his stature should give a more broad picture of the Jews around them rather than letting Fagin stand alone as "the Jew" (Johnson, 1010–12). Dickens responded in two ways: for the 1867 Charles Dickens edition of *Oliver Twist* he altered a number of references to "the Jew" to "Fagin" or "he," and in *Our Mutual Friend* (1864–65) he took pains to present a kindly Jewish character.

Fagin, as Dickens so unhesitatingly and instinctively presented him, bore many of the characteristics of earlier literature's stereotyped Jew. As Edgar Rosenberg has noted, Dickens portrayed the Jew in his two dominant criminal guises, "the twin roles of mutilator and usurer," in which he had been typecast since medieval days. For Rosenberg, although Fagin's profession ties him to the nineteenth century, his Jewishness is less specifically that of Dickens's immediate observation than a "dehistorized" association of Fagin "into some prehistoric fiend, an ageing Lucifer."[37]

We see Fagin mostly through the perspective of Oliver, who regards him less particularly as Jew than as a nightmare figure, dark and diabolic. When Oliver first hears of him from the Artful Dodger, he learns that Fagin is an "old gentleman," a term Dickens's first readers would have immediately associated with the "old one," the devil. The first view of him, old and shriveled with a "repulsive face . . . obscured by a quantity of matted red hair," and subsequent mention of him as "loathsome reptile" and as having "fangs such should have been a dog's or rat's" further such impressions.

This combination of associations produces a kind of "distorted dream-figure" or "grotesquely magnified bogey out of a fairy-tale" (Rosenberg, 119). But this distortion gains particular force precisely because the novel's opposing and long-impotent powers of goodness also come across as dreamlike and distant—prophesied by the dying Little Dick, immortalized in a long-unrecognized portrait, remembered finally by the Oliver who can revisit a past that has been purged of its uncertainties and threats. The sources and uncertain powers of evil are no better defined than the sources and powers of goodness in this novel, but the powers of evil seem more immediate because they are the more active and assertive powers for so much of the story. Graham Greene has well described this situation in noticing "the different levels of unreality in this closed Fagin universe," and he finds himself wondering whether Dickens's appeal comes from his unconscious attention to "the eternal and alluring taint of the Manichee, with its simple and terrible explanation of our plight, how the world was made by Satan and not by God, lulling us with the music of despair" (1951, 57).

Certainly were Fagin simply the stereotypical Jew, or the criminal of popular fiction, or the snarling villain of melodrama, we would find him entirely forgettable. But the prevailing sense of him—both Oliver's and ours—is that he cannot be known so easily. He is best seen as least seen, as a man with little or no past, without a full name, hidden but never housed until finally imprisoned, motivated ostensibly by greed and the desire for power but clearly the victim of his own uncertainties. He thus is the composite of all that cannot be comprehended, and that is not a bad definition of a "bogey-man."

After the long comic scene in which Oliver is introduced to the gang and trained as a pickpocket, there are few times when Fagin is present for long, and Oliver only knows what Fagin is not—not the respectable gentleman or mere miser that he has called himself, but a fence and thief. With Oliver we well may continue to wonder just who Fagin is—a recurrent nightmare, put away only through public exposure, judgment, and the sentence of death, a process itself filled with potential nightmare.

Fagin's powers for so much of the story depend on secrecy. He must not be found; he must be on the move; he must anticipate trouble, and he is remarkably good at it. When observed, he controls what is seen through the play of his "games" with the boys, his explanations of himself as "mere miser" after the half-conscious Oliver sees him with his open strongbox. The underworld depends on Fagin's skills at deception and concealment; he is a sort of magician as was Dickens (literally in his love of conjuring games and figuratively in his storytelling). The entire plot, as we later learn, is to discredit Oliver, if not to corrupt him at least to make him appear corrupted, to disprove his right to an inheritance and to the confidence Brownlow was initially so ready to have in him. Thus John Bayley finds Fagin's wish to incriminate Oliver to be "an objective and social terror as well as a psychological one" (1962, 446).

So outlined, *Oliver Twist* sounds like the old story of the good guys fighting the bad guys for the prize, which here happens not to be the girl but the parish boy who must himself be proven worthy of the property. Such a reading misses what I think is the most fascinating quality of this novel, its hesitancy to come to terms with just who Fagin is, how certain anyone can be of him. The critical moments come not when Oliver is in his clutches but when he seems most protected from Fagin. Recuperating in the country with the Maylies, Oliver appears secure in a fresh and tidy world so far from the dirt and frightening underworld as to render it an impossibility:

> The little room in which he was accustomed to sit, when busy at his books, was on the ground-floor, at the back of the house. It was quite a cottage-room, with a lattice-window: around which were clusters of jessamine and honeysuckle, that crept over the casement, and filled the place with their delicious perfume. It looked into a garden, whence a wicket-gate opened into a small paddock; all beyond, was fine meadowland and wood. There was

no other dwelling near, in that direction; and the prospect it commanded was very extensive. (ch. 34)

The novel's opposed worlds uncannily coalesce, because Oliver soon finds himself in the same state of mind—or, more accurately, mindlessness—that he had experienced his first morning in Fagin's den. Dickens stresses the uncertainty of Oliver's consciousness, but waking or sleeping the boy finds himself in a state of heightened awareness:

> There is a drowsy state, between sleeping and waking, when you dream more in five minutes with your eyes half open, and yourself half conscious of everything that is passing around you, than you would in five nights with your eyes closed, and your senses wrapt in perfect unconsciousness. At such times, a mortal knows just enough of what his mind is doing, to form some glimmering conception of its mighty powers, its bounding from earth and spurning time and space, when freed from the restraint of its corporeal associate. . . .

> There is a kind of sleep that steals upon us sometimes, which, while it holds the body prisoner, does not free the mind from a sense of things about it, and enable to ramble at its pleasure. . . . It is an undoubted fact, that although our senses of touch and sight be for the time dead, yet our sleeping thoughts, and the visionary scenes that pass before us, will be influenced, and materially influenced, by the *mere silent presence* of some external object; which may not have been near us when we closed our eyes: and of whose vicinity we have had no waking consciousness. (chs. 9, 34)

Seldom, especially in these early years of his career, does Dickens so explicitly consider the workings of the mind, and in much of the rest of his characterization of Oliver he fails to make the boy even interesting, much less capable of such heightened awareness. But by twice commenting on Oliver's visions while asleep or nearly asleep and by having both of these involve Fagin, Dickens affirms the near simultaneity of dream and nightmare as well as of reality and imagination. The text's illustration showing Fagin and Monks at the window while Oliver dozes in his chair notwithstanding, we are left with the sense that the idea of Fagin and his cohorts may be more terrifying than their actual presence, and when Oliver and his friends find no traces of them, we shudder at their intrusion into what had promised to be an inviolable Eden.

Secretive, protective of his powers, Fagin is always more ready to spy than to be spied upon. Not only does he watch the sleeping Oliver, but later when Noah Claypool comes to London he first spies on him from a peephole in a public house and later sends him to watch Nancy. It is appropriate, then, that the terms of Fagin's undoing are ones of exposure, much of which he suffers and some of which we participate in through our last view of him in Cruikshank's famous illustration "Fagin in the Condemned Cell." His troubles begin, as he realizes, when Nancy overhears him plotting against Oliver. To avenge her having disclosed their hiding place "and where it could best be watched from," Fagin tells Sikes of her betrayal, begging him not to be too violent. As the day breaks in this scene, however, Fagin and Sikes see one another's faces: "there was a fire in the eyes of both, which could not be mistaken" (ch. 47). Thus Fagin becomes party to the murder, and, like Sikes, he will be exposed and have the sense of many eyes on him. At his trial he feels himself "surrounded by a firmament, all bright with gleaming eyes." He notes in the courtroom an illustrator (Cruikshank perhaps?) dispassionately "sketching his face in a little note-book" (ch. 52). The psychology of exposure works well here to reverse the terms of Fagin's success as a criminal. He had kept himself obscure, a point reinforced by having few of the illustrations show his eyes; at the trial and in the condemned cell, however, he is seen wild-eyed with terror. Desperate, he sits "awake, but dreaming," and his guard, although used to such sights as his "paroxysm of fear and wrath," realizes that "one man could not bear to sit there, eyeing him alone; and so the two kept watch together" (ch. 52).

Here once more the relationship of subject and object have been reversed as the man who once watched the sleeping boy now finds himself the object of observation. For Oliver, life at least had remained uncertain with shadowy figures, but for Fagin, the gallows has become his only certainty. Although Oliver faints as he leaves Fagin's cell, the visit has for him confirmed the resolution of a major question of his story—it is Fagin, not Oliver, who is doomed. All the early joking about the gallows as the destiny of the

"Fagin in the Condemned Cell." *George Cruikshank illustration.*

bastard child has proven false; all the banter among the thieves about their reaching "the top of the tree" (becoming the master criminal) has come to "the cross-beam, the rope, and all the hideous apparatus of death" (ch. 52).

To so notice the changing perceptions of and by Fagin is to acknowledge this book's linking of the powers of life and death, although not necessarily to agree with Graham Greene's reading of this as a Manichaean world, because the sources and nature of Fagin's power, while often seeming diabolical, remain obscure and generally uncertain. If the "good" world, and Oliver in particular, somehow "needs" a Fagin in the way a theology may need a devil to cast out, control, or overcome, then for a number of reasons this Fagin "needs" an Oliver. This is very much a story of possession—literally through its attention to wills and inheritances and rightful versus fraudulent ownership of property, but more figuratively through its attention to people's powers over one another. Just as in other ways he had irked the authority of the beadle, Oliver immediately presents a challenge to Fagin. Here is the boy of all boys to train for a criminal career, for this boy, unlike the others, does not look the part. Here, as Fagin instantly recognizes, is the morality to "poison"—perhaps because it is so innately pure but certainly because it is so much fun to play with. Dickens's handling of this struggle may often seem pure melodrama, but the psychology is sound as he stresses the delight Fagin takes in telling Oliver "stories of robberies he had committed in his younger days: mixed up with so much that was droll and curious, that Oliver could not help laughing heartily, and showing that he was amused in spite of all his better feelings" (ch. 18). Dickens was neither the first nor last to present the devil as an entertainer, and he may have inadvertently opened up the question of how readily the entertainer may be devilish.

As Fagin works to win over Oliver, his ultimate purposes are very serious. He wants not just the boy's services but his heart and soul, and for a while it looks as though the odds are in his favor: "Having prepared his mind, by solitude and gloom, to prefer any society to the companionship of his own sad thoughts in such a dreary place, he was now slowly instilling into [Oliver's] soul the poison which he hoped would blacken it, and change its hue for ever" (ch. 18). So committed, Fagin is working (as always) as much for himself as for Monks, and if I am at all a typical reader, I am not surprised that I pay little attention to the complicated explanations of Monks' having used Fagin for his revenge against Oliver's family. The fascination Fagin has in trying to possess Oliver for his own irrational ends remains motive enough.

As some of Cruikshank's unpublished sketches for the final installment suggest, Dickens may have remained uncertain about what to do with Fagin until soon before finishing the book. Among the Cruikshank papers remain sketches of Bill Sikes in the condemned cell. Had Dickens, at his own or Cruikshank's instigation, not determined to bring the Fagin story to its climax with prison and gallows, we well wonder what he might have done with it. The uncertainty may have remained for so long because just as Fagin had so protected himself and so insinuated himself psychologically in this novel's worlds, the novelist too might naturally resist his exposure and end.

9

Oliver?

Because of the musical comedy *Oliver!*, which had a long run in London and New York and became an Academy Award–winning film, many people over the last 25 years have become familiar with Dickens's *Oliver Twist* without ever having read it. The frequently revived musical, as the exclamation point of its title signals, presents a most upbeat version, one that might have been written by the Artful Dodger himself. To consider the popular stage and film musical as part of a history of adaptations that began even before the first serialization of Dickens's novel was completed, I have changed the exclamation point of the musical's title to a question mark, because this stage and screen version, especially, raises the question of just how adaptation affects our understanding of *Oliver Twist*.

For the reader more interested in Dickens's novel and what has happened to it than with the purely theatrical or cinematic quality of the adaptation, a play or film based on the novel becomes a "reading" of the novel. Like the Cruikshank illustrations accompanying the serial, and like Dickens's subsequent "Sikes and Nancy" reading, an *Oliver* play or film puts the book newly before the audience's eyes and ears. In the case of silent film, with its much abbreviated text on screen, the visual effect is one of greatly expanded and suddenly animated illustration. In sound films an instrumental score is often added, with much greater audio effect coming in the song and dance of the musical versions. So considered, "adaptation" is necessarily elaborative, for when the written word is spoken, the described scene presented, and the narrated story acted, the text undergoes fundamental changes as the new presentation itself becomes an interpretation, a reading. This may be more evident when we consider what is lost or endangered when a novel becomes the basis for a play or movie.

For novel readers, adaptations often lack completeness, because the stage or film version may have fewer characters, omit subplots and shorten the main story, or alter the story significantly. Certainly such productions as those broadcast on public television's Masterpiece Theatre or the Royal Shakespeare Company's epic *Nicholas Nickleby* are more complete and elaborate than other adaptations, but even such faithfulness to detail may seem strangely incomplete. The reader confronts the particular magic of the written work differently when read silently rather than when heard or seen. Fictions build the sense of completeness through conjuring acts of making readers believe in the first place that print on a page is life itself, that imagined characters are themselves speaking, acting, and imagining lives that began before the opening pages and that continue after we leave them. For example, when we begin *Oliver Twist* we do so with the implicit awareness that Bumble has been about his business of naming and abusing workhouse boys for some time, that there is a story beginning before young Oliver's birth (something much more particular than the "same, old story" so prejudicially ascribed to his anonymous mother by the parish authorities). Similarly, at novel's end we are given every assurance that life in England will go on for Oliver, and perhaps somewhere else for the Artful Dodger, his comic counterpart.

Such patterns follow the formulaic "once upon a time" and "ever after" of conventional storytelling, and certainly these also are strong stage and film conventions, especially in the melodramatic earlier adaptations of *Oliver*. The point, however, is that in the course of reading a novel these assumptions and expectations sustain suspension of disbelief over the long haul of reading and help build the reader's confidence in the story's context in times and places beyond the limits of its published beginning and ending.

In the shorter duration of a play or film the trade-off may be for the greater immediacy provided by the visual and spoken work, with the dramatist, scriptwriter, and actors doing the interpreting.

Yet even these versions can naturally expand the narrative beyond the confines of the stage or screen. For example, when Lon Chaney or Alec Guinness plays Fagin or when a famous child actor plays Oliver, the knowledgeable film audience associates this performance with the actor's roles before and after *Oliver Twist*. But the key difference about the "life" so acknowledged beyond the single representation is that it often involves the interpreter's history beyond the performance (a demonstrably "real" history, albeit one of various enactments) as well as the totally imagined history the text itself may project backward and forward in time.

Such expansions of the audience's sense of completeness in reading or in watching a play or film version raise some essential issues of fictional representation. I have earlier used the word "magic," have spoken of fiction's "conjuring acts" (incidentally, Dickens loved to play the magician to his children). The great achievement of the English novel of the eighteenth and nineteenth century was its illusion of realistic representation, particularly its persisting argument that it was providing a full and authentic account of human experience. Obviously such phrases as "full and authentic," particularly in definitions of "human experience," are problematic, and every reader of a Dickens's novel soon encounters unresolved tensions between the realistic and the fantastic. Dickens saw himself as part of a novelistic tradition committed to completeness of representation and insisted, as in the 1841 Preface to *Oliver Twist*, that what he had written was "true." Here is the magic of the novelist, the "realizing" of the imagined and the imagining of the real. When it works, such representation tricks us into believing what "occurs" in the course of the parish boy's adventures. Stage and film adaptation, then, provides a repetition of the initial representation: a stage or film "version" may please or displease us according to how faithfully it repeats the novel for us. But as the very word indicates, an "adaptation" changes the original, and the move from print to stage or screen necessitates projection and interpretation as the new representation itself becomes for us a part of the fiction's afterlife.

Even before finishing his story, Dickens recognized his novel's theatrical potential. He was only about halfway along with his serial in March 1838 when to his actor friend Frederick Yates he proposed "to dramatize Oliver for the first night of next Season"

(*Letters*, 1: 338). The editors of Dickens' letters are unable to date this proposal completely, but they presume it came before Dickens learned of the first pirated dramatization of the novel on 27 March 1838, and they note that five different versions were performed before Yates finally staged it on 25 February 1839 (*Letters*, 1: 388). It was not uncommon for Dickens to object to stage versions and to printed parodies or imitations of his works coming forth before his serials were complete, but it was unusual for him to propose a stage version of a work in progress. In this instance he tried to outdo his pirates and imitators, for, as he told Yates, his popularity as author and Yates's as a well-known actor playing Fagin "would knock any other attempts quite out of the field." Yates later did play Fagin and his wife played Nancy, but Dickens did not himself write the adaptation, although he evidently sanctioned it. As Peter Ackroyd has remarked, the novel seemed ready-made for adapters, "who merely excised the social criticism and cut down the plot," allowing them to hit audiences "with a fresh blast of life and truth."[38]

Dickens, however, stated his "general objection to the adaptation of any unfinished work of mine, . . . that being badly done and worse acted it tends to vulgarize the characters, to destroy or weaken in the minds of those who see them the impressions I have endeavoured to create, and consequently to lessen the after-interest in their progress" (*Letters*, 1: 463). Dickens's first concern was protection, for both his profits and the integrity of his work, but his comments also point to the central questions of adaptation—especially the focus on particular characters and the fidelity of the adaptation to the impressions and themes Dickens developed through characterization.

Every adapter of *Oliver* must determine how to present the title character and Fagin and also how closely to follow the book's story line. Early stage versions often used women in the title role, and this concerned Dickens, who found one of the actresses "many sizes too large." He thought that if the role had to be played by a female (women often played children's parts in the nineteenth century), "it should be a very sharp girl of thirteen or fourteen" (*Letters*, 1: 388). The earliest stagings obviously could not accurately anticipate subsequent developments of an unfinished novel, and thus

Dickens had particular reason to fear their vulgarizing and distorting his work.

Even when working from the completed text, adapters greatly altered *Oliver Twist* as they focused on major characters, reduced the number of characters, and simplified the complicated plot. If, as Dickens's choice of Yates indicates, an adaptation is to be the vehicle for a well-known actor, then a single role stands out more on stage than it did in novel because of the theatrical need to keep that character on stage as much as possible. Films, through deft cuts from scene to scene, may accommodate larger casts, but even the film versions of *Oliver* capitalize on the name value of the stars, whose stature affects the adaptation's focus. Concerning a *David Copperfield* adaptation a commentator once quipped that the film raised the question of whether W. C. Fields was playing Mr. Micawber or Micawber was playing Fields, and Lon Chaney's, Alec Guinness's, Jackie Coogan's, Ron Moody's, or Dickie Moore's appropriations of the *Oliver Twist* characters raise similar questions. Whether in cameo or lead roles, actors have provided unforgettable renderings of Dickens's characters; given the comic potential of Bumble, however, it is surprising that his has not become a particularly memorable part on stage and screen, at least not until the full measure of his pomposity emerges through his operatic posturings in the musical.

The familiarity performers may give to Dickens's characters is not simply that which they bring as a Guinness or Chaney or Coogan but is a result of superb casting, interpretation of speech and gesture, and of makeup and costuming that makes their roles readily recognizable. Dickens wrote for an audience who read novels aloud, and thus his characters are as vocal as any in fiction. Ways of speaking, details of appearance, particular gestures keep individual characters distinct as they reappear during long months of serial publication. The Dickens characters became more distinct through the illustrations that accompanied each monthly part, and the memorable George Cruikshank illustrations forever determined the physical appearance of the stage and film characters, particularly Fagin, Bumble, and Sikes, and they also gave clear direction to the setting of the major scenes.

A dramatic adaptation of the novel thus becomes an extension of the illustrations, and just as the illustrations can capture only parts of the novel even as they focus on key people and moments, so too do adaptations become necessarily partial in their representations of Dickens. Textual purists may call for such totalities as the Royal Shakespeare Company's eight-hour stage production of *Nicholas Nickleby* or the BBC's 12-part television production of *Oliver Twist*, but many less complete renderings of Dickens have succeeded because they have so well captured the essential theatricality of his fiction, in which the part suggests the whole.

Although less than two hours in duration, the 1922 silent film of *Oliver Twist* (with Jackie Coogan as Oliver and Lon Chaney as Fagin) adheres to the novel remarkably well; even with very little print appearing on screen, it serves as an interpretive summation. It is serious and straightforward in presenting the deprivations of Oliver in the workhouse and in Sowerberry's coffin room ("a gloomy bedroom," declares the caption). With swift, skillful cutting it captures the novel's juxtapositions of respectability and underworld, especially when, at the climax, the camera moves from a touching picture of Oliver sleeping securely at Brownlow's to an anxious Nancy waiting in her bed before Bill Sikes returns to murder her. These work so well because the film has carefully prepared the audience by earlier showing Oliver in much less easy repose and by tracing Nancy's increasing sympathy for him.

Few subsequent film versions attend as carefully as does this one to Oliver's differing degrees of consciousness. Here we see him as sleeping infant, hungry boy dreaming of food (the picture superimposes stick figures of a bowl and spoon dancing over his body), unconscious during the charade of justice by the magistrate, and having nightmares about Fagin and the gang while away from them. At such moments the silence of the silent film works to great advantage. The Oliver in this film acts more assertively than does the novel's hero, for once inside the house at Chertsey he tries to thwart the robbery, and in a greater distortion of the ending he begs leniency for Monks, with the caption stating, "Oliver bows in thanks to the man who has apprised him of his true name—Oliver Leeford."

Except for giving the title character more prominence and life than he often has in the novel, this film is remarkably faithful to Dickens's work, for it effectively opposes different scenes and sets of characters to suggest the precariousness of Oliver's life. Chaney's Fagin is sinister and certainly sets the mode for subsequent actors' interpretations of that role.

The first sound film version (with Dickie Moore as Oliver, Irving Pichels as Fagin, and William Boyd as Sikes), a 77-minute feature, appeared in 1933. In the wake of Coogan's silent-film performance, Moore's is the lead role in this production, which truncates and alters the story to downplay Bumble, eliminate the Sowerberry episode, and redefine Rose Maylie as Brownlow's niece. In this version Oliver's mother turns out to have been married, and Nancy is known as "Nancy Sikes" whereas the silent film had introduced her unabashedly as "Sikes's woman."

Fagin in the silent film had conspired with Monks to keep Oliver "under wraps," and that film altered the setting to bring Sikes back to Fagin's den before he jumps to his death. Fagin then is hauled along the street by a mob, and we see him again briefly in the condemned cell. The 1933 film shows him with head wrap and scowling, and it repeats the silent film's shot of his capture and end in the condemned cell, but on the whole the character is less vividly rendered than was Chaney's "crafty, old shriveled scoundrel," who first appeared as gap-toothed, hunched, with skullcap, as he admired sketches of the gallows.

David Lean's 1948 feature film remains the most controversial of the *Oliver* films, largely because of its depiction of Fagin. As a whole, however, the film conveys more emphatically than any other the novel's connections between criminality and poverty. As in Lean's earlier *Great Expectations*, the black and white visual impact is striking, here capturing the atmospheres of workhouse, Sowerberry's shop, and Fagin's London. As in the novel, the film's aura of terror seems more authentic than does its satirical or romantic elements, perhaps because the final 15 minutes or so greatly condense the second half of the novel, in which the romantic resolution was so lengthy. The film completely eliminates the Maylies, makes Brownlow Oliver's grandfather, and has Brownlow replace Rose as Nancy's confidant. It suggests a more evil Artful Dodger by transferring to him Noah Claypool's function as Nancy's betrayer.

After Oliver flees to London, this film belongs to Fagin and Sikes, with few hints of a comic or sympathetic Fagin. The 1922 and 1933 versions showed Fagin at play with the boys as he trained Oliver to pick pockets, and the 1933 film had a touching scene in which Fagin provided a steaming plate of food to the weary Oliver. But Alec Guinness, made up with an enormous nose, long hair, and a beard and talking with an unmistakably Jewish accent, emphasizes the character's sinister side, and, as the negative reaction from both European and American audiences indicated, the anti-Semitism with which Dickens himself had been charged flared again. For some, the release of the film in 1948 was too close to the Holocaust, and a 7 March 1949 *Life* magazine article, "Fagin in Berlin Provokes a Riot," described two nights of protest before the film was withdrawn from a West Berlin theater. Guinness's Fagin, with "lisping, rasping speech and oily, mincing mannerisms," resulted in the film's being banned in the United States until 1951. Even then, some 11 minutes, mostly close-ups of Fagin, were expurgated, and a complete version was not shown in America until 1970.[39]

Dickens, as I noted in Chapter 8, first defended his characterization of Fagin as realistic, because, as contemporary records indicate, Jews often were fences. But more than 25 years after writing the novel he became aware that Jewish readers had taken offense, and he accordingly eliminated many references to Fagin as "the Jew," although he did not change any of his speech or mannerisms, and the Cruikshank illustrations had by then fixed Fagin's physical description. It was Lean's fidelity to the Cruikshank illustrations and to the Dickens characterization that, more than 100 years after Dickens, provoked so much revived criticism about anti-Semitism.

The problem thus is not a new one, and in fact comes up in other versions when we encounter racism or sexism in literature from other times. Uncertain what readers in the 1990s might make of the Lean film's Fagin, I recently asked undergraduates to view it and respond. One student, Bryan Levinson, had been cast as Fagin in a school play years before. At the time he had thought little of it, but later he realized that he had probably been given the role because he was Jewish. Yet when he wrote for a class paper about Guinness's controversial portrayal, Levinson made an interesting defense of the image as "part of Fagin":

> It is the part of a tradition that had grown over centuries. The anti-Jewish feel of Fagin is the result of a cultural bias that affected the viewpoints of Dickens, Cruikshank, and later inter-

pretations of their work. But that viewpoint must be respected in a cultural context of the past. . . .The wrong thing to do is to suppress the image from the past for fear of what it means today. The image from the past did not necessarily hold the same meaning as it does in the present. The ban of David Lean's *Oliver Twist* kept the audience from confronting the historical view of the Jew. We must understand the bias and background of that vision and how it differs from the one we know today. To delete from history what we find offensive is the most dangerous act of all.[40]

The frankness of this film is evident also in its handling of Bill Sikes's murder of Nancy, for unlike other adaptations it shows the murder and follows the terror-stricken Sikes during his flight, making a point of his unsuccessful effort to destroy his dog.

British television productions of classic novels often have great advantage over feature films because they recapture both the serial structure through their part presentations and the fullness of the original through their total length. In 1985 the BBC produced a 12-part *Oliver Twist* featuring Eric Porter as Fagin. The part divisions stand well as units, and by close attention to character and incident, the novel's many themes and moods emerge. The opening segment starts with the baby's howling, and with a masterful portrayal of Bumble's naming of Oliver and subsequent reacquisition of him from the baby farm. So Bumblesque is this rendition that the audience might mistake the beadle's seemingly Christian resignation as genuine when he remarks to Mrs. Mann, "Its the Lord's will that so many go into his hands." Soon, however, we see he is the hypocrite who starves boys while lecturing on the sin of greed. No other stage or film version so fully presents the workhouse and the heartless rationale of the poor law, and to stress the point the film shows the burial of a dead workhouse boy on a cold, snowy day.

Complete with coffin snuffbox, Mr. Sowerberry appears at the beginning of the second television installment, and embellishing the Dickensian phrase, he cannily states that for him "every tear is another shilling in the till." His spouse here seems more the sadist than either in the novel or previous adaptations, for she makes Sowerberry flog Oliver.

Subsequent installments take Oliver to London. The Dodger he meets there seems singularly shabby, Nancy particularly alluring, and Fagin especially insecure. As in the novel, this Fagin clearly is on the watch rather than in control, and although he is often vicious, the characterization downplays his Jewishness. Behind him lurks a Monks remarkably true to Dickens's original, for he is subject to fits, reacts wildly when lightning strikes, and makes a point of displaying the odd scar beneath his chin.

The scope of this adaptation provides opportunities for a number of parallels, and one that works effectively throughout involves various couples—Bumble and Mrs. Mann (and subsequently Mrs. Corney), Bill and Nancy, Charlotte and Noah, the Sowerberrys. Set against these often grotesque relationships, the love story of Rose and Harry and the yearnings of Oliver for family, especially for his mother, become understandable if sentimental.

As a late-twentieth-century adaptation, this version is interested in the characters' states of minds and motives, but unlike some Dickens's adaptations—such as a 1970s *David Copperfield* that transformed Dickens's innocent hero into a more modern existential sufferer—this *Oliver* includes but does not exaggerate the novel's occasional attention to the workings of memory, dream, and imagination. Thus it well represents the times when Oliver is uncertain whether he is dreaming or awake, Nancy's realization of her inexplicable attraction to Bill ("I am drawn back to Bill even if I should know I was to die by his hand"), and the strange power over Oliver of the lady's portrait in Brownlow's sitting room.

The production's final installment, which is generally faithful to the novel's prolonged conclusion, curiously does not include Fagin's trial but leaves him condemned and madly raving that he yet has papers that will prove Oliver's identity. The film does well in explaining that Rose's history, as well as Oliver's, was part of Monks's secret, because just as it was in his interest to discredit his half-brother so had his mother started the story that Rose was illegitimate.

Like the stage productions, most films of *Oliver Twist* are limited by severe time demands, but, like the Royal Shakespeare Company's *Nicholas Nickleby* and the stunning two-part feature film of *Little Dorrit*, the BBC's serial production provides novel readers with the most complete dramatization of Dickens's novel. The success of such works makes one wonder whether it will again ever be possible for a film to succeed in the more limited terms of the effective silent movie or powerful David Lean adaptations of *Oliver*.

Dickens's fiction inspired song and dance in his day, and in recent years *Pickwick*, *Quilp (The Old Curiosity Shop)*, *A Christmas Carol*, and *Drood* have appeared as full-scale musicals, but none has had the popularity of Lionel Bart's *Oliver!*, which ran for 2,618 London performances after opening in June 1960.[41] It enjoyed a successful New York run and has been revived several times. Carol Reed's 1968 film of this musical won five Oscars and a number of international awards and is now available on videocassette. Although visually it may owe something to earlier *Oliver Twist* films, this is an adaptation of a stage adaptation, and the conventions of stage musical are often at odds with the Dickens material. The videocassette case in fact acknowledges that the musical is "freely adapted from Charles Dickens's *Oliver Twist*."

The musical largely ignores the film tradition that, with varying success, had sought to replicate Dickens's self-conscious realism, to animate scenes and characters as they are in the novel, and to reiterate his sense of social injustice, tentative providence, and relish for the grotesque and terrible. On the other hand, the musical builds on an aspect of Dickens that may be less prevalent or less appealing in the written text of *Oliver Twist* than in such other works of his as *A Christmas Carol* or *David Copperfield*—his sentimental comedy, buoyant spirit, and persisting faith in the prevalence of goodness. In these respects, Dickens was an ancestor of the mid-twentieth-century musical comedy, and modern readers will hardly be surprised to learn of Dickens's own lifelong pleasure in attending, writing, and sometimes participating in various musical performances. It is on this side of Dickens that *Oliver!* capitalizes, and its great popularity with stage and screen audiences certainly parallels much of Dickens's popularity with his first readers. It is easy for Dickens purists to complain and even sneer at the musical, and in passing remarks in early chapters I probably have done so. I was concerned, however, that if a reader comes to the novel after having seen the musical version, he or she may be ill-prepared for the novel's mixture of the serious and comic, the realistic and fantastic, and for its fascination with the underworld, especially the violence lurking in Fagin, Sikes, and Monks. The novel, as I have repeatedly argued, is preoccupied with the weight of the past and the uncertainty of the present, and it takes considerable special pleading to conclude with a more promising future. Instead, the musical is a world of greater positive energies, even though it preserves the same story elements of workhouse, undertaker's shop, thieves' den, and murdered mistress.

Absent from the musical is the darkness that the black and white films, like Cruikshank's illustrations, so highlighted. Absent, too, is much of the squalor and desperation of life. Even the boys parading into the workhouse refectory *look* well fed as they receive their meager gruel, and they certainly have plenty of energy for singing and dancing. Fagin and his boys, though shabby, also have great energies, and even their London seems surprisingly bright and clean.

Many modern musical scores focus on the sportive and the sentimental, with fast-paced numbers and dazzling choreography exaggerated through various camera techniques alternating with a sentimental ballad as theme song, often in solo or duet, such as Oliver's "Where Is Love?" or Nancy's "He Needs Me." A cue for the musical's playful numbers (invariably with much running and leaping) comes from the novel's incident where Oliver first watches and then joins in Fagin's "game" of training the boys to pick pockets. Even the most serious film versions often caught the inherent comedy of this moment when Fagin masquerades most blatantly as a "respectable gentleman" target for his charges, and Oliver, yet totally unaware of the company he has joined, thinks it all great fun. The musical's memorable rendition neatly captures all this, and in addition it totally transforms Fagin's rationalizations of his profession into a modern tradesman's ethic, "You've got to pick a pocket or two."

Ron Moody as Fagin retains only a few of the marks of the original or of the many stage and film portrayals of this character. He is red-bearded, often dressed to resemble the Fagin who became familiar from Cruikshank's drawings, and when we first meet him he has toasting fork and sausage in hand. But this is a bright-eyed and fast-footed Fagin, a man more often than not enjoying life, and as active singer and dancer he seems a far cry from the skulking, insecure figure of Dickens's novel, where even in the illustrations his eyes were usually hidden. Moody's Fagin does have his moments of fear as when he finds Oliver watching him with his treasure, when he fears that Oliver will inform the magistrate or Mr. Brownlow about himself and the gang, but the Moody characterization reveals little of the more paranoiac Fagin of novel and many films.

But just at the point where viewers familiar with Dickens's novel or with the earlier films may begin to think that the musical has eliminated all the darkness and violence of *Oliver Twist*, Bill Sikes appears. We see first a monstrous shadow of an approaching man; then Bullseye, his dog, emerges from an alley, followed by Sikes himself. As he comes toward a tavern, Nancy is finishing her first song, "It's a Fine Life," and the mood suddenly changes. Throughout this scene Bill never speaks until Nancy follows him out, and then he speaks only to his dog, calling him to come along. Sikes is the only major character never to have a musical part in *Oliver!*, and thus he is a threatening outsider to its world. He lurks in its gardens, tries to break into its houses, and he literally takes Fagin by the throat. The musical eliminates the novel's principal villain, Monks, and self-protection is the only apparent motive for Bill's insistence that Fagin and Nancy recapture and retain Oliver. But this characterization of Sikes highlights one of the book's major points, Nancy's realization of her fatal attraction to Bill, which comes across poignantly in her song "He Needs Me." Understanding the strangeness of her devotion, she declares, "I feel inside the love I have to hide. . . . I know where I must be."

For all her commitment to Sikes, the musical's Nancy takes on a more active role toward the end than did the character in the novel. After Sikes and Oliver return from an unsuccessful attempt at housebreaking, Nancy orchestrates a vigorous tavern dance number to distract Sikes while she steals Oliver away to deliver him to Mr. Brownlow on London Bridge. (An audience familiar with another popular musical of the 1960s, *The Sound of Music*, may find a parallel with the pageant scene where the family distracts the Nazis in order to flee the country.) This change in the *Oliver Twist* story economizes the novel's more sprawling ending because it keeps Nancy and Oliver together in the moments before her death and his rescue. Bill follows them from the tavern, seizes and beats Nancy to death near the bridge and makes off again with Oliver. Brownlow and a crowd soon follow, and Oliver is freed only after Sikes is shot while trying to escape across the rooftops.

Meanwhile, Fagin and the boys have determined "to change lodgings," and, rather than have the angry crowd capture Fagin as many of the film versions concluded, the musical's Fagin is last seen on a street leading toward a bridge with bright light on the other side. He has dropped his jewel box in the muck and seems headed toward a path of reform until the Dodger appears and presents him with a freshly picked purse, and they skip off together, singing to the tune of "Reviewing the Situation," that "once a villain, a villain to the end" and concluding that they are "living proof that crime can pay."

As such musicals as *West Side Story, Les Miserables,* and *The Phantom of the Opera* also demonstrate, a written story's atmosphere and themes may be translated into visual, vocal, and kinetic forms. In regard to faithfulness to an original from which a musical is however "freely" adapted, the challenge is to avoid the silliness of the music hall on the one hand and the overstatement of the opera on the other. I have said that for all its changing of Dickens's story and especially its conversion of Fagin into capering trickster, the musical *Oliver!* often projects the cheery, bustling Dickens world. As did the films featuring child movie stars, this version supports the novel's emphasis on little Oliver's sturdy spirit. One magnificent production number midway through the musical effectively places Oliver as engaged spectator of the wondrous world of Dickensian joy. He has been brought to Brownlow's after having been proven innocent of theft, and he awakens to a marvelous street scene that opens with flower girls and milkmaids singing, "Who Will Buy My Red, Red Roses." Soon all of respectable London seems to appear—a knife grinder, sets of schoolchildren, businessmen off to their jobs, servants and their mistresses—and the dance concludes with a military band marching down the street. It all has something of the Disneyland parade, to which Oliver remains the engaged spectator, adapting the tune to ask, "Who will buy this wonderful feeling; I'm so high I could fly."

This part of the musical is noteworthy because, in presenting a scene for which the novel gave no suggestion, it concentrates all the positive Dickensian energies, is true to the musical convention of such production numbers (there is at least one similar scene in *Mary Poppins*), yet for the reader comparing novel with musical it is a reminder of the liberties this adaptation has taken with Dickens's story.

A key moment in the novel comes when Oliver, as secure in the Maylies' country cottage as the musical's boy is at Brownlow's, sits at his desk dozing. In the background of Cruikshank's famous illustration we see Monks and Fagin leering in at Oliver through an open window. Dickens's commentary leaves uncertain whether Oliver wakes or dreams, but he certainly is shaken with the thought that his security is so threatened. In the musical number we again see an Oliver in the home of friends, but this time he is certainly wide awake and eagerly watching the entertaining spectacle in the street, and he certainly does not see Sikes and the Dodger lurking in the park, and for that matter we do not see them either, until a brief shot reveals their silent presence and then the film cuts back to them at Fagin's, where they scheme to recapture Oliver. As in the musical's characterization of Sikes, the evil, so often more problematic and therefore threatening in the novel, is less immediately part of Oliver's consciousness, and thus those of the audience interested in comparing title character of musical and book might want the exclamatory title *Oliver!* changed to a querying *Oliver?*

notes

1. Preface to the 1841 edition of *Oliver Twist* (New York: Penguin, 1988), 33–37; hereafter cited in text as "1841 Preface."

2. The most complete discussion of the women in Dickens's life and fiction is Michael Slater's *Dickens and Women* (Stanford, Calif.: Stanford University Press, 1983).

3. "A Preliminary Word" to *Household Words*, vol. 1 (London: Bradbury & Evans, 1850), 1.

4. John Forster, *The Life of Charles Dickens*, vol. 1 (Philadelphia: J. B. Lippincott, 1886), 57; hereafter cited in text.

5. Madeline House and Graham Storey, eds., *The Letters of Charles Dickens*, vol. 1 (Oxford: Clarendon Press, 1965), 231; hereafter cited in text as *Letters*.

6. Henry Mayhew, *London Labour and the London Poor* (1861; New York: Dover Publications, 1968), title page; hereafter cited in text.

7. Catherine Gallagher, "The Body versus the Social Body in the Works of Thomas Malthus and Henry Mayhew," in *The Making of the Modern Body: Sexuality and Society in the Nineteenth Century*, ed. Catherine Gallagher and Thomas Laqueur (Berkeley: University of California Press, 1987), 91.

8. John Roach, *Social Reform in England, 1780–1880* (London: B. T. Batsford, 1978), 116.

9. Steven Marcus, *Dickens: From Pickwick to Dombey* (New York: Simon & Schuster, 1965), 60; hereafter cited in text.

10. London *Times*, 8 August 1834; articles hereafter cited in text as *Times* followed by date of publication.

11. Robert A. Colby, *Fiction with a Purpose: Major and Minor Nineteenth-Century Novels* (Bloomington: Indiana University Press, 1967), 124.

12. Charles Shaw Lefever, Charles Roman, and Edwin Chadwick, *First Report of the Constabulary Commission* (London, March 1839); hereafter cited in text.

13. Review reprinted in *Charles Dickens: The Critical Heritage*, ed. Philip Collins (London: Routledge & Kegan Paul, 1971), 73; hereafter cited in text.

14. *Oliver Twist*, ed. Kathleen Tillotson (Oxford: Clarendon Press, 1966), 398–400.

15. Review (*Quarterly*, 1837) reprinted in Collins, ed., *Critical Heritage*.

16. David Paroissien, *Oliver Twist: An Annotated Bibliography* (New York: Garland, 1986), 102.

17. Review reprinted in Collins, ed., *Critical Heritage*, 83–86.

18. Fred Kaplan, *Dickens: A Biography* (New York: William Morrow, 1988), 507.

19. Philip Collins, ed. *Sikes and Nancy: A Facsimile* (London: The Dickens House, 1982); hereafter cited in text as *SN*.

20. J. Hillis Miller, *Charles Dickens: The World of His Novels* (Cambridge: Harvard University Press, 1958), 36.

21. See "The Young Dickens" in Greene's *The Lost Childhood and Other Essays* (London: Eyre & Spottiswode, 1951); hereafter cited in text.

22. Years later, beginning another new project, the Urania Cottage home for fallen women, Dickens said he would undertake direction of the institution "with my whole heart and soul" (*Letters*, 4: 555).

23. Edgar Johnson, *Charles Dickens: His Tragedy and Triumph* (New York: Simon & Schuster, 1952), 193; hereafter cited in text.

24. Janet Larson, *Dickens and the Broken Scripture* (Athens: University of Georgia Press, 1985), 49.

25. See also Richard J. Dunn, " 'But We Grow Affecting: Let Us Proceed,' " *Dickensian* 62 (1966): 53–55.

26. Charlotte Brontë, *Jane Eyre*, ed. Richard J. Dunn (New York: W. W. Norton, 1987), ch. 24.

27. James Kincaid, *Dickens and the Rhetoric of Laughter* (Oxford: Clarendon Press, 1971), 69.

28. William T. Lankford, " 'The Parish Boy's Progress': The Evolving Form of *Oliver Twist*," *PMLA* 93 (1978): 26.

29. Quoted in Fred Kaplan, *Dickens and Mesmerism* (Princeton, N.J.: Princeton University Press, 1975), 52. Kaplan notes that while writing this part of the novel, Dickens had been a frequent observer of a mesmerist who believed that the mesmerized subject could see with eyes closed.

30. Quoted in *Two Reminiscences of Thomas Carlyle*, ed. John Clubbe (Durham, N.C.: Duke University Press, 1974), 136.

31. Joseph M. Duffy, Jr., "Another Version of Pastoral: *Oliver Twist*," *ELH* 35 (1968): 419.

32. There has been considerable commentary about Cruikshank's interest in Fagin. See Richard A. Vogler, "Cruikshank and Dickens: A Reassessment of the Role of the Artist and the Author," *Princeton University*

Library Chronicle 13, no. 44, 61–91; Jane R. Cohen, *Charles Dickens and His Original Illustrators* (Columbus: Ohio State University Press, 1980), 15–38; Michael Wynn Jones, *George Cruikshank: His Life and London* (London: Macmillan, 1978), 59–79.

33. Wynn Jones includes the illustration on p. 72.

34. G. K. Chesterton, *Charles Dickens: The Last of the Great Men* (New York: Readers Club, 1942), 81. First published in 1906 as *Charles Dickens: A Critical Study.*

35. John Bayley, "*Oliver Twist*: 'Things as They Really Are,' " in *Dickens and the Twentieth Century*, ed. John Gross and Gabriel Pearson (London: Routledge & Kegan Paul, 1962), 53.

36. Robert Tracy, " 'The Old Story' and Inside Stories: Modish Fiction and Fictional Modes in *Oliver Twist*," *Dickens Studies Annual* 17 (1988): 115.

37. Edgar Rosenberg, *From Shylock to Svengali: Jewish Stereotypes in English Fiction* (Stanford, Calif.: Stanford University Press, 1960), 118.

38. Peter Ackroyd, *Dickens* (New York: HarperCollins, 1990), 27.

39. Jerry Vermilye, "*Oliver Twist*" in *The Great British Films* (Secaucas, N.J.: Citadel Press, 1978), 117–120.

40. For a listing of commentary on the Lean adaptation of *Oliver Twist*, see David Paroissien, "*Oliver Twist*": *An Annotated Bibliography* (New York: Garland, 1986), 73–83.

41. For a listing of musical numbers and adaptations of *Oliver Twist*, see Paroissien, *An Annotated Bibliography*, 83.

selected bibliography

PRIMARY WORKS

The Letters of Charles Dickens. Edited by Madeline House and Graham Storey. Oxford: Clarendon Press, 1965–. This in-progress edition is the standard edition of Dickens's letters; it greatly expands the three-volume Nonesuch edition of 1938.

Oliver Twist. Edited by Kathleen Tillotson. Oxford: Clarendon Press, 1966. An excellent introduction. Describes in detail the novel's composition, publication, and revision.

Oliver Twist. Edited by Angus Wilson. New York: Penguin, 1966. This edition indicates the original part divisions by asterisks at the end of each part.

Sikes and Nancy: A Facsimile. Edited by Philip Collins. London: The Dickens House, 1982. Provides a firsthand view of Dickens's final work with *Oliver Twist*.

SECONDARY WORKS

Biographies

Ackroyd, Peter. *Dickens*. New York: HarperCollins, 1990. The most detailed of the Dickens biographies; attempts "to incorporate all known material on the life of Charles Dickens."

Forster, John. *The Life of Charles Dickens*. 3 vols. London: Chapman & Hall, 1872–74. Although surpassed in many ways by more recent biographies, Forster's is the firsthand account by a close friend of Dickens.

Johnson, Edgar. *Charles Dickens: His Tragedy and Triumph*. 2 vols. New York: Simon & Schuster, 1952; rev. ed., New York: Viking Penguin, 1977. A very readable biography focusing on Dickens as social critic, popular entertainer, and a man beset by conflicting emotions.

Kaplan, Fred. *Dickens: A Biography.* New York: William Morrow, 1988. Supplements Johnson and effectively positions Dickens among his many associates as the best-known writer of his time.

Criticism: Books

Chittick, Kathryn. *Dickens and the 1830s.* Cambridge: Cambridge University Press, 1990. A detailed study of the relationship between Dickens's early journalism and fiction. Through her survey of some 800 contemporary reviews Chittick provides a full account of the reception of Dickens in the 1830s.

Cohen, Jane R. *Charles Dickens and His Original Illustrators.* Columbus: Ohio State University Press, 1980. Well summarizes what can be determined about the controversial claims George Cruikshank made about his part in *Oliver Twist.*

Collins, Philip. *Dickens and Crime.* London: Macmillan, 1968. A study of Dickens's life-long interest in crime and criminals; particularly useful in understanding Dickens's fascination with the underworld in *Oliver Twist.*

_____. *Dickens: The Critical Heritage.* London: Routledge & Kegan Paul, 1971. Reprints four early reviews of *Oliver Twist.*

Ford, George H. *Dickens and His Readers.* Princeton: Princeton University Press, 1955. Ford's is an engaging account of Dickens's phenomenal popularity; his consideration of *Oliver Twist* well relates that novel to the writer's other early successes.

House, Humphry. *The Dickens World.* London: Oxford University Press, 1941. One of the best resources for the connections between what Dickens wrote and the times in which he lived; useful for the social and historical background of *Oliver Twist.*

Larson, Janet. *Dickens and the Broken Scripture.* Athens: University of Georgia Press, 1985. A thorough study of the modifications Dickens made for his own time of *The Pilgrim's Progress* through the allusion of his subtitle "The Parish Boy's Progress."

Marcus, Stephen. *Dickens: From Pickwick to Dombey.* New York: Simon & Schuster, 1965. Marcus's discussion of *Oliver Twist* ("The Wise Child" and "Who Is Fagin?") and his appendix on Fagin are important modern readings, connecting the novel with a tradition of parables, envisioning "a world in which the good heart carries everything before it, . . . a world in which the self finally undercuts society itself."

Miller, J. Hillis. *Charles Dickens: The World of His Novels.* Cambridge: Harvard University Press, 1958. Influential in the shaping of modern Dickens criticism, Miller's study regards Oliver's world as "an imaginative complex of claustrophobia" from which there is no escape.

Patten, Robert. *Charles Dickens and His Publishers.* Oxford: Clarendon Press, 1978. Discusses the contractural details of *Oliver Twist* and provides information about its sales.

Slater, Michael. *Dickens and Women.* Stanford, Calif.: Stanford University Press, 1983. This extensive study of Dickens's relationships with women and of his fictional women provides much useful information about his characterization of Nancy and of Rose and about how his young sister-in-law's death influenced *Oliver Twist.*

Criticism: Articles and Parts of Books

Bayley, John. "*Oliver Twist:* 'Things as They Really Are.' " In *Dickens and the Twentieth Century,* edited by John Gross and Gabriel Pearson. London: Routledge & Kegan Paul, 1962. Challenging both those who stress the novel's fidelity to the actual or its mythic view of life as imprisoning, Bayley argues for its liberating fantasy, which leaves key characters "free in spirit and in impulse against all physical and factual likelihood."

Dickens Quarterly 4 (1987). *Oliver Twist* 150th Anniversary Issue. Contains articles on the novel's economic ideas, illustrations, "religious romanticism," language of doubt, stage and screen adaptations, and influence on the role of the orphan child in later fiction.

Duffy, Joseph M., Jr. "Another Version of Pastoral: *Oliver Twist.*" *ELH* 35 (1968): 403–21. Finds Brownlow and Fagin to be antagonists struggling for control of the title character, who is "an emblem of vulnerable and threatened innocence."

Greene, Graham. "The Young Dickens." In *The Lost Childhood and Other Essays,* 51–57. London: Eyre & Spottiswode, 1951. Like Bayley, Greene notices the novel's "levels of unreality," principally in Fagin's closed universe.

Lankford, William T. " ' The Parish Boy's Progress ' : The Evolving Form of *Oliver Twist.*" *PMLA* 93 (1978): 20–32. Examines the author's struggles to evolve a narrative form for rendering "the compulsions of his imagination and the truth about his society."

Rosenberg, Edgar. "The Jew as Bogey." In *From Shylock to Svengali: Jewish Stereotypes in English Fiction,* 116–37. Stanford, Calif.: Stanford University Press, 1960. An extensive discussion of the antecedents in fiction and drama and also of Dickens's more personal sources for the characterization of Fagin.

Tracy, Robert. " ' The Old Story ' and Inside Stories: Modish Fiction and Fictional Modes in Oliver Twist." *Dickens Studies Annual* 17 (1988): 1–33. In an essay that could serve as an excellent introduction to the novel, Tracy discusses a number of forms of story and storytelling to conclude that "Dickens has made his subject the processes and metaphysic of fiction itself."

Bibliography

Pariossien, David. *Oliver Twist: An Annotated Bibliography.* New York: Garland, 1986. Provides a remarkably full description of the novel-in-progress, the novel's historical background, and information on such related studies as the poor laws. Lists stage, film, musical, and television adaptations along with contemporary reviews and criticism.

index

Index

the author

Richard J. Dunn is professor of English and associate dean for humanities at the University of Washington in Seattle. A former president of the Dickens Society, he has taught Dickens at the U.S. Air Force Academy, the University of Colorado, in a London study-abroad program, and to undergraduates and graduates at the University of Washington. He has edited *David Copperfield: An Annotated Bibliography* (1981) and *Approaches to Teaching Dickens's "David Copperfield"* (1984), as well as critical editions of *Jane Eyre* (1971, 1987) and *Wuthering Heights* (1990).